HAVING WORKED WITH hundreds of sales forces across every industry, we have seen the world's top salespeople in action. Chally's research truly captures the skills, behaviors, and habits of the best of the best . . . and most interestingly, through the eyes of the customer. *Achieve Sales Excellence* should help every salesperson enjoy the high-value, enriching profession that sales has become for the world-class sellers portrayed in this book.

Steve Grossman
Mercer Human Resource Consulting

ONE OF OUR KEY DIFFERENTIATORS at CareerBuilder.com is our salespeople's ability to be consultants to our customers. We also pride ourselves on the quality standards we set for our own salespeople. Our demand for professionalism is exceptional and we are hard to please. *Achieve Sales Excellence* is not only a real benchmark for our high standards; it's thoroughly enjoyable to read. I usually only agree to 20–50 percent of the philosophies in sales books but with *Achieve Sales Excellence* I agree with it all!

Mary Delaney
CSO, CareerBuilder.com

CORPORATE EXPRESS IS COMMITTED to enhancing our customer-focused sales-driven organization, and the principles and tactics outlined by Chally are key strategies to our success. Chally's World Class Sales Research recognizes and defines the key attributes that create a world-class sales organization—attributes that all companies should strive for when augmenting their sales culture.

Donna Walker
Vice President, Sales Operations and Training
Corporate Express

IT SEEMS A BUSINESS PARADOX that a professional discipline as important as sales is given so little attention in college and university curriculums. HR Chally helps to fill that void with a clear, concise insight into "world class sales" of the 21st century. If sales growth is important to you . . . this information is invaluable.

Tom Weisenbach
Senior Vice President, International Paper
Executive Vice President, xpedx

CHALLY HAS LED THE WAY to understanding the need to develop a true sales profession. More college graduates are becoming salespeople than any other career, regardless of their major. Other key business careers such as manufacturing, IT, and now even law are moving abroad. Sales has become our key competitive opportunity. *Achieve Sales Excellence* definitively documents the standards our salespeople must meet, and lays the foundation for our academic institutions to develop the sales professionals we'll need.

Don Graber
Chairman, Wright State University
Chairman, Huffy Corporation, Retired

ACHIEVE SALES EXCELLENCE

THE 7 CUSTOMER RULES FOR BECOMING
THE NEW SALES PROFESSIONAL

HOWARD STEVENS
CHAIRMAN AND CEO OF THE HR CHALLY GROUP

AND THEODORE KINNI

PLATINUM
PRESS™

AVON, MASSACHUSETTS

Published by
Platinum Press™, an imprint of Adams Media,
an F+W Publications Company
57 Littlefield Street, Avon, MA 02322. U.S.A.
www.adamsmedia.com

ISBN 10: 1-59337-651-0
ISBN 13: 978-1-59337-651-2

Printed in the United States of America.

J I H G F E D C B A

Library of Congress Cataloging-in-Publication Data
Stevens, Howard
Achieve sales excellence / Howard Stevens and Theodore Kinni.
p.   cm.
Includes bibliographical references and index.
ISBN-13: 978-1-59337-651-2
ISBN-10: 1-59337-651-0
1. Industrial marketing. 2. Customer relations. 3. Customer loyalty.
4. Selling—Study and teaching. I. Kinni, Theodore B. II. Title.
HF5415.1263.S84 2007
658.8'04—dc22
2006032596

This publication is designed to provide accurate and authoritative information with
regard to the subject matter covered. It is sold with the understanding that the
publisher is not engaged in rendering legal, accounting, or other professional advice.
If legal advice or other expert assistance is required, the services of a competent
professional person should be sought.
—From a *Declaration of Principles* jointly adopted by a Committee of the
American Bar Association and a Committee of Publishers and Associations

Many of the designations used by manufacturers and sellers to distinguish their
product are claimed as trademarks. Where those designations appear in this book
and Adams Media was aware of a trademark claim, the designations have been
printed with initial capital letters.

This book is available at quantity discounts for bulk purchases.
For information, please call 1-800-289-0963.

Contents

The Greater Goal

This book is dedicated to the great progress we need to make toward the "professionalization" of sales, and also to those who have had the insight and commitment to champion this transformation. Today, more college graduates will become salespeople than all other careers combined. Yet fewer than a couple dozen of the more than four thousand colleges and universities in the United States have established a formal sales program.

I have been honored to be involved with the Sales Centre at Ohio University and the other colleges of the University Sales Center Alliance. One hundred percent of Chally's profits from this book will be contributed to them.

It will take an effort from our great colleges and universities to create the three minimum requirements for "professionalization":

1. All professions specialize. Chemical engineers do not design bridges, pediatricians don't do brain surgery, and patent attorneys don't defend murder cases.

   Chally's research has identified fourteen distinct types of sales. The skills and training for each are distinct. Most are not interchangeable. The great majority of New Business

Developers (Hunters) fail at Account Maintenance (Farming). Field Sales people seldom succeed in telesales, and so on. In fact, 65 percent of the salespeople who fail do not fail from lack of competence or commitment; they fail because they are in the wrong type of sales for their talent and skill base.

2. All professions have a standard and recognized minimum "curriculum" of academic education, on-the-job training, or internship. Members of professions also benefit from the appropriate practice through supervised apprenticeship that oversees the quality of their development and maturity as practitioners.

3. All professions have an independent "certification" process that anoints the emerging intern or student as minimally qualified to practice their chosen profession.

In the meantime, corporate sales organizations must fill the gap with the help of sales training resources. Unfortunately, only a few non-college sales development organizations have recognized the hands-on participatory requirement for the "training" of sales professionals.

Through this book, Theodore Kinni and I seek to honor such visionary leaders as Richard Hodge of the Real Learning Company. Richard was one of the first to recognize that while people are appreciative or even impressed with experts and by interesting and entertaining seminars and sales training programs, they only absorb and utilize the insights and skills they personally choose for themselves, through discussion, debate, and hands-on "testing."

Finally, this book is dedicated, most of all, to the wisdom, scientific competence, and statistical insight of Sally Stevens, without whom there would not be a thirty-year database with hundreds of thousands of actuarially predictive data points, nor the database mining and retrieval technology that makes Chally's one of the world's half dozen or so true blue "Expert Systems."

Howard Stevens

The New Sales Profession

S alespeople, by and large, are not the business partners that their customers need them to be. For all of the effort salespeople invest in becoming valuable business partners, they are still often regarded as product pushers or "talking brochures" who consume, not create, value.

In this book, Howard Stevens and Theodore Kinni address this problem by exposing the sources of the sales-customer disconnect. *Achieve Sales Excellence* provides amazingly clear insight into the minds of business-to-business customers—insights that most salespeople will find both believable and compelling. If you are committed to becoming a world-class seller, this book could be the launching point for the rest of your career.

The Sales Force Paradox

There is a fundamental paradox within sales forces. The paradox has probably always existed, but it has become more pronounced and more troubling as the relationships between buyers and sellers have become increasingly complex. It is a paradox that keeps most salespeople from blowing past their goals and attaining their envisioned riches. It is a paradox that frustrates customers and encourages them to view salespeople as a nuisance to be avoided at all costs.

The fantastic paradox goes something like this: Sales forces around the world enjoy remarkably frequent and intimate contact with their customers. Remarkable as it is, a few assumptions and simple math tell us that there are literally billions of sales calls made each day around the world. Salespeople are, by definition, the customer's primary point of contact throughout the customer's buying process, so no one inside a company should know as much about customers as the sales forces that serve them.

Ironically, though, those exact sales forces do not understand the true needs of the very customers they face countless times a day. No, we're not implying that they don't understand their customer's immediate *business* need for a particular product or service—good salespeople are experts at finding the precise offering that will fill a customer's current business requirement. The need that salespeople can't see, *despite* their frequent and intimate contact with customers, is one that goes to the core of their very existence. Frankly stated: Most salespeople do not understand why their customers need *them*!

The salespeople who *have* been able to decipher the buying needs of their customers are the superstars. Their customers adore them, and these salespeople enjoy extreme customer loyalty. They are referred to their customers' peers and receive unencumbered access to every level of the organization. They have resolved this sales paradox, serve their customers exactly as they want to be served, and earn the label of world-class sellers.

The majority of salespeople, however, remain unenlightened and continue to sell the way *they themselves* believe their customers want to be served. These are the salespeople who consistently fall short—not only in the eyes of their managers, but also in the eyes of their bewildered customers. These salespeople often lament that "customers don't have time for salespeople any more." Well, unfortunately for them, customers *do* have time for world-class salespeople, just not for salespeople who don't provide the value that customers demand from today's sales professional.

When *Learning* from the Past Dooms You to Repeat It

So what is it about this profession of selling that makes it so difficult? Well, as is pointed out in the first chapter of this book, there is something unique about the sales domain—something that is different from every other profession. There is no real "curriculum" or baseline education for salespeople. Attorneys have law schools where they learn legal statutes and precedents. Accountants attend colleges where they learn the Generally Accepted Accounting Principles. Engineers attend universities where they learn the laws of physics.

So what do salespeople have by way of education? They have mostly tribal knowledge that is passed down from generation to generation of salespeople. "This is how I closed the biggest sale of my life," or "This is the cold calling script that works every time," or some other anecdotally derived wisdom that succeeded for someone in the past. Whether taught in the office by peers, in hotel ballrooms by sales trainers, or in books by salespeople turned gurus, there is little knowledge in the sales domain that can be trusted as law or science—at best, there are "generally accepted principles." But alas, there is no foundational sales curriculum.

But let us be fair to the generations of salespeople who *did* close those big sales and *were* excellent cold callers. There is another unique thing about the profession of selling . . . It is in a constant state of change. With every advance in telecommunications (cellular phones and the Internet), every change in business models (outsourcing and globalization), and every swing of the economy (recessions and booms), the relationships between buyers and sellers change dramatically. Did it make sense to teach salespeople closing techniques when most salespeople sold products? Sure. Did it make sense to teach cold calling when buyers still answered their telephones? Of course. Does it make sense to teach accounting now that ROI is the key to an executive's heart? Absolutely.

The point is the rules of engagement in sales are everchanging. If they weren't, all that worked in the past would indeed predict success in the future. If the sales environment were static, all of the anecdotal success stories would eventually accrue to become immutable law. But it is not that simple in sales. As the world changes, so do the demands on the sales professional. And so, we are trapped in this paradox. We sell to our customers as best we can, using the grab bag of skills we have learned as journeymen in the sales profession.

What If?

But what if there were a way out of this paradox? What if we could climb inside the heads of our customers to discover what they really want from us? What if we could track in real time the changes in their buying needs, instead of always selling a generation behind? What if there were a contemporary "curriculum" for achieving world-class status in the eyes of our customers?

Well . . . Here it is. The book you hold in your hands is as close to a curriculum for business-to-business selling as there has been in decades. This book can help you escape the paradox and become indispensable partners to your customers by understanding the precise things your customers need from you. It is different from the dozens of others on your shelf in two critical ways—two ways that make it a touchstone for business-to-business selling in the twenty-first century.

Foremost, this book is not based on the anecdotal successes of superstar salespeople. It is not based on the "tricks of the trade" of any celebrity salesperson turned guru. In fact, not a single salesperson was interviewed or observed as an input to this book. In reality, salespeople do not define the characteristics of world-class sellers . . . Buyers do. Accordingly, Howard Stevens and his researchers at Chally went straight to the source to discover why customers need salespeople—they asked the customers themselves. The findings in this book are based on over 80,000 interviews with business-to-business customers. The interviews were solely focused on isolating and prioritizing the discrete things that buyers want and need from the sellers who serve them. (In fact, we know of only two sales research efforts ever conducted in this depth and to this level of analytic rigor: HR Chally's current fourteen-year 80,000-customer interview study and Neil Rackham's twelve-year 35,000-sales call study that led to the *SPIN Selling*® methodology. These are both phenomenal commitments to the betterment of the sales profession.) This book is not tribal knowledge; it is fact.

Second, this book is not a history lesson. It is relevant for today's sales forces in today's business environment. The research that you will see in the following chapters has been collected at regular intervals for a decade, allowing the HR Chally team to track buying and selling trends as they have evolved with our economy. All of the major changes that have redefined the nature of selling (information technology, ubiquitous communications, outsourcing, globalization, focus on ROI, etc.) have come into bloom under the watchful eye of Chally's researchers. Not only do these findings hit the mark in 2006, they also reflect the insights of marksmen who have followed the moving target for fourteen tumultuous years. At this point in time, there is no more authoritative work on the demands of business-to-business buyers than the book that you are about to read.

And Here We Are

Bluntly, the profession of selling is not where it needs to be. As you will discover in the following pages, there exists an enormous gap between our customers' *demand* for world-class salespeople and our sales forces' ability to *supply* them. Howard Stevens and his team at HR Chally Group very concisely define the nature of this gap and give us guidance on how to begin closing it.

So for now, the fog has been lifted and we can see with clarity why business-to-business customers need professional salespeople. It is the most rigorous, comprehensive, and trustworthy perspective that we have had in decades. Treat this book as a modern-day sales curriculum, and take its lessons to heart. Your customers and your bank accounts will thank you, as you and the members of your sales force become the world-class salespeople that your customers need you to be.

Jason Jordan
Principal
Mercer Sales Effectiveness Consulting

Note: Mercer's Sales Effectiveness consultants help clients create world-class sales efforts by developing the right sales strategies, customer focus, management processes, and infrastructure to meet or exceed their key revenue and profit objectives. Their clients enjoy greater top-line growth, lower cost of sales, and more predictable results through improved selling capabilities and management practices. They are a part of the Human Capital business of Mercer Human Resource Consulting, the global leader for trusted HR and related financial advice, products, and services, with more than 15,000 employees in forty-one countries worldwide. To learn more about Mercer, visit *www.MercerHR.com.*

Introduction

What qualities define sales excellence?
What capabilities define the highly effective sales professional?
What are the characteristics of a world-class sales force?

If you are pursuing or considering a career as a professional in sales, these three questions are critical. Many people have already attempted to provide answers to them. In fact, as of December 2005, Amazon.com listed an astounding 194,945 titles in the "Selling" category. Virtually all of them promise to answer one or more of these questions. When examined from a scientific perspective, however, virtually all of the publications have two inherent flaws.

First, the answers they offer cannot be validated; that is, they are based on anecdotal evidence or the author's experience, and cannot be proven. Second, they do not account for the inexorable march of time. Change happens, and when it does, it often transforms even the most rigorous conclusions into hogwash. To overcome these critical flaws, you need empirical answers and you need them on an ongoing basis.

At the HR Chally Group, a leading sales performance consulting company, we have been intensely interested in the answers to these three critical questions for virtually our entire thirty-three-year history. After all, we could not be sure we were actually helping our clients select the best candidates for their sales forces unless we had a validated, criteria-based method for evaluating those candidates. To properly define the testing criteria, we needed hard answers to these questions both for the marketplace as a whole and, more specifically, for our individual clients' markets.

Starting in 1992, we stepped up our search for answers. We began a series of studies, now in their fourteenth year, which focused on the best source of empirical data about the effectiveness of salespeople that we could tap—the business-to-business customers who buy from those salespeople. In the process of conducting these studies, which continue as this book is written, we have interviewed 80,000 business customers and collected data on 7,200 sales forces representing more than fifteen major industries. We asked these customers to rate between two and five individual salespeople (by market segment) who were actually competing for their business. Our research does not rely on customer opinion alone, however. We correlated the customers' ratings of salespeople against their actual purchasing decisions for the current year of the survey and for previous years, as well as against their estimates for the coming year. In this way, we began to uncover what drives repeated decisions to buy (or, to put it another way, "customer loyalty"), as well as individual purchases.

As you will see in Chapter 1, our Customer-Selected World-Class Sales Excellence surveys revealed that customers assign salespeople a much larger role in their buying decisions than has been previously realized. We also discovered that customers believe that the vast majority of salespeople are not able to fulfill that role as well as customers would like. There is, in fact, a wide and largely unbridged Sales Effectiveness Gap.

The purpose of this book is to help you bridge that gap. In order to accomplish that goal, the first thing you need to know is what business customers really want from their vendors. We'll help you answer that question in Chapter 2. In it, we describe the three megatrends that business customers identify as driving their relationships with vendors: first, the intense desire to outsource everything except core competencies; second, the overwhelming demand for solutions rather than products and services; and third, the drive to achieve value. It is these three trends that establish the context of today's business-to-business sales environment. They are also the driving forces behind the customer rules that you will read about in this book.

These customer rules are the seven expectations that customers have of salespeople. The rules constitute the heart of *Achieve Sales Excellence*, and we describe them in detail in Chapters 3 through 9. The rules are not a simple wish list that business customers have dreamed up and that we are quoting to you verbatim. Instead, they represent the customer demands *that have been correlated to their actual purchasing behavior.* The rules determine from whom and how much your customers actually buy. The customer rules provide empirical customer answers to the first question we asked in this introduction: *What qualities define sales excellence?*

In describing the qualities of sales excellence, the customer rules also define the skills that customers expect sales professionals to bring to the table. Thus, each of the customer rules is connected to a corresponding role for the sales professional, and, in Chapters 3 through 9, we'll present these roles as well. In order to illustrate the seven roles, we've utilized the final element of our research—the benchmarking data gathered from our studies of sales forces that business customers have identified as world-class, and the data derived from HR Chally's proprietary database of more than 300,000 sales professional profiles. This is the largest known database of individual sales profiles in the world, and it too is correlated against the actual sales results of the individuals included within it. This is how we derive empirical answers to the second question of critical interest to sales professionals and their managers: *What capabilities define the highly effective sales professional?*

The Customer Rule	The Sales Professional's Role
"You must be personally accountable for our results."	The Business Agent
"You must understand our business."	The CEO
"You must be on our side."	The Advocate & Expediter
"You must bring us applications."	The Consultant
"You must be easily accessible."	The Traveler
"You must solve our problems."	The Troubleshooter
"You must be innovative in responding to our needs."	The Innovator

Finally, in Part Four, we'll use the data gathered in our benchmarking studies to describe the eight characteristics of sales forces that customers define as the best of the best. This section frames the answer to the last question *(What are the characteristics of a world-class sales force?)* in terms of eight evaluative questions. If you are a sales professional—in particular, one who is following the seven customer rules—you can use these questions to help choose an employer who will best recognize and appreciate your capabilities. If you are a sales manager, you can use these questions to ensure that you are properly supporting the daily and developmental needs of your salespeople. And, if you are an executive, you can use them to evaluate your company's ability to meet the demands of customers, as well as to attract and retain the best sales professionals.

Our primary goal in this book is to educate sales professionals about the skills they must develop to succeed with customers, *and* also teach them how to identify sales organizations in which they can prosper. Our secondary aim is to inform sales managers and executives about the skill set they need to develop in their sales forces, as well as the organizational qualities they need to develop to serve customers and attract the best salespeople. We hope you will find all the answers you need in the pages to come.

PART ONE

What Good Science Reveals about Sales Excellence

There are many theories purporting to predict sales success, and more seem to be emerging every day. The problem with all theories is that, in and of themselves, there is no way of knowing whether or not they are accurate and/or able to predict results. They must be rigorously tested and empirically proven.

At the HR Chally Group, we learned this lesson early in our history. We were founded to help create consistent, legally defensible assessments of job candidates. In business, if you have a fifty-fifty chance of picking a good employee and you use an assessment that raises your odds to sixty-forty, that is a significant improvement. Then, one day, the Justice Department hired us to create an assessment for selecting law enforcement officers. These were people who were being issued guns and given the authority to use them. Accordingly, we realized we had to create an assessment with much higher levels of predictability.

The first thing we did in that quest was to turn to widely accepted standard tests and assessments, such as personality, style, aptitude, preference, and even interest tests. These only allowed us to gain prediction improvements of 8 percent to 14 percent. We then carefully and statistically created new tests based on psychological theories, such as Maslow's hierarchy of human needs, Herzberg's motivational theory, and McClelland's achievement theory. When we tried out these tests, however, we quickly discovered that they could not tell us, with the accuracy we needed, which candidates would succeed and which would not.

Next, we looked for predictability models that were already working. We found two. You can accurately predict results based on mathematical odds—just look at the gaming industry. You also can accurately predict results based on criteria-based actuarial studies; that is the basis for the insurance industry. Of course, we adopted the latter method.

There is a problem with criteria-based prediction, however. The results you get are only as good as the criteria you use. With law enforcement officers this was not a huge problem—their performance records are highly detailed and, in most cases, meticulously maintained. But when we began assessing salespeople, the performance criteria were not so easy to identify.

We tried enlisting sales managers to help us identify the criteria that define sales success, but that strategy did not work. Sales managers had little disagreement in determining the top 10 percent and the bottom 10 percent of salespeople. But we discovered an insurmountable problem with the remaining 80 percent. It turns out that managers prefer salespeople who are easy to manage. So, in the vast middle range of salespeople, higher performers who are hard to manage and lower performers who are easy to manage often get ranked about the same. Anyone who has met more than a few good salespeople can tell you that they usually are not the most manageable of people. This bias explains why sales managers can often be poor measures of sales talent.

Finally, we did discover an excellent source for criteria to predict the success of salespeople beyond their actual sales results (which are sometimes not completely the result of their own skills). This was their customers. Customers could tell us why they buy from salespeople and why they do not, and we could validate their criteria for sales success by correlating it to the share of their wallets that they awarded those salespeople.

Good science has enabled us to recognize and pinpoint sales excellence. Also, in studying the customer's buying behavior to pinpoint the criteria that determine sales excellence, we got the added bonus of learning more about why customers buy, and what they want.

In Part One, we will begin by introducing the most significant finding that our customer studies have revealed over the past fourteen years. We will also explain what customers want, and we'll introduce the seven customer rules, which dictate the skills you need to develop to achieve success.

CHAPTER 1

The Sales Professional *Is* the Sale

What's the most influential factor in business-to-business sales? It isn't competitive pricing. It isn't your product's Six Sigma quality. It isn't your product's innovative features or your company's ability to deliver a total solution. Certainly all of these influence your customers' buying decisions, but surprisingly, none of them is the *most* influential factor in their decisions. The most influential factor in business-to-business sales is *you*—the sales professional.

You don't have to take our word on this; it is business customers themselves who have placed salespeople in the top spot. Since 1998, our statistical analysis of purchasing decisions has demonstrated that the sales professional is the most important factor in determining what customers purchase, how much they pay, and how long they stick with the lucky vendors they choose from the thousands of business-to-business sellers competing for their patronage. In fact, our analysis proved that salesperson effectiveness accounts for 39 percent of customers' buying decisions and is the most important decision factor—more influential than price, quality, and the availability of a total solution.

This is a notable development in the sales world, and it represents the ascension of a new competitive advantage in the business-to-business sphere. Sales professionals have become the leading influence on their customers' buying processes—more important than the selling price, more important than the offering's features and benefits, more important than the product and service quality. This means that the effectiveness of sales professionals themselves can be an added value to their customers and a competitive advantage for their employers. In the 1960s, media guru Marshall McLuhan declared that the medium is the message. Now, in the business world, the salesperson is the sale.

What's Important When Customers Choose Their Vendors
Salesperson's competence: 39%
Total solution: 22%
Quality of offering: 21%
Price: 18%

An Evolutionary Pattern of Development

When did this change happen? Our in-depth vendor evaluation interviews with more than 80,000 business customers first revealed in 1998 that in their estimation, the salesperson had ascended to the top position of influence. This did not occur overnight, though, nor has it completely eclipsed the other influencing factors in the business-to-business sale. Instead, it is an evolutionary development that has been building momentum for years.

The nature of competitive advantage in sales has always been evolutionary. That is why other factors have been more important than sales effectiveness in customers' buying decisions in the past. Product and service quality is a good example. Quality became a primary concern of business-to-business customers in the late 1970s and 1980s as well-made and dependable

Japanese and German automobiles and electronics captured market share from their American competitors. As U.S. manufacturers lost customers, they became aware of the magnitude of the costs they incurred from product defects and failures, and, even more important, aware of the customer defections and lost sales that poor quality engendered.

The ensuing focus on—and demand for—greater levels of quality spawned a revolution. Quality-based concepts and programs, such as Total Quality Management (TQM), kaizen, just-in-time inventory systems, the Malcolm Baldridge National Quality Award, and ISO 9000, dominated the corporate landscape. American companies worked hard and invested significant capital in their efforts to improve the quality of their products. They demanded that their suppliers do the same. Vendors and their sales forces quickly responded to these demands and began winning business by demonstrating the high quality of their offerings and guaranteeing continued quality.

As soon as product and service quality proved capable of winning business, the quality competition really heated up. Sellers strove to match and exceed the quality of their competitors' offerings. As a result, quality levels are much higher today than they were in 1980. Six Sigma programs, whose goal is the achievement of a de facto defect rate of 3.4 per million opportunities, are now the quality programs du jour. Theoretically, this standard represents the lowest defect rate that is economically worthwhile to attain.

But what has happened to quality as a competitive advantage in sales during this time? In the years between 1980 and the widespread adoption of Six Sigma, the differentiation power and competitive advantage of product and service quality have been slowly and inexorably reduced. Today, the quality of your products and services is considered a baseline requirement rather than a competitive advantage. You can't win or retain customers without high-quality products and services, but neither can you win based on quality alone. Every viable competitor is offering high quality, and customers' standards and expectations regarding quality have risen accordingly.

In most industries, trying to gain a competitive advantage by offering a higher level of quality simply doesn't make sense. The difference between a few handfuls of defects spread over a million parts isn't economically compelling to customers. Thus, as quality standards have risen and been matched by more and more competing vendors, quality has lost its power as a competitive advantage and has been transformed into an ante that is required to gain a seat at the table.

Sales effectiveness, which is based on the competence of the salespeople and the resources and support provided by their companies, is subject to the same evolutionary pattern as is quality. It has risen to the top of the customer's influence list because demand is far outstripping the supply. Today, the customer's need for a competent, professional salesperson has grown well beyond the ability of salespeople to fulfill it and, all the evidence suggests, will continue to grow as far into the future as we can see.

To help understand the driving force behind this condition (and the critical and largely unfulfilled role that customers want salespeople to assume), we need only take a step back and start by acknowledging a very basic fact: The only reason a corporate customer buys anything is because his company cannot or chooses not to make or provide it for itself. If the customer's company *were* making or providing it, it would have its own internal organization to do that work *and*—this is the key part—it would have a manager or executive responsible for that function. That is to say, it would have someone who was accountable for ensuring that the company actually received the benefit that the product or service was designed to provide. Thus, a business customer's decision to buy a good or a service externally is not simply a decision to purchase—it is also a decision to outsource the management of the benefit that the purchase is intended to deliver.

What does mean for you, as someone trying to sell to that company? What we have discovered is that business customers are turning to salespeople to fulfill the role of surrogate manager. When salespeople become adept at managing the total benefit delivered to their customers, the supply will meet the demand. At that point, sales effectiveness will decline as a competitive advantage, just as quality has. Someday, if enough salespeople and companies recognize and build their sales effectiveness, it may only count as a portion of the entry fee. But today, as we'll soon see, the research reveals that fewer than one out of a thousand salespeople can perform to this level!

While the power of salesperson effectiveness to influence customers may eventually decline, there are two reasons no salesperson or sales organization can afford to ignore it now or in the future:

First, whether it is a full-blown competitive advantage or simply the table stakes required to enter the game, sales effectiveness will remain a critical ingredient in sales success. In the former case, it is a scarce and in-demand expertise that will help you achieve above-average sales results. In the latter case, when customers simply expect you to possess that expertise, you won't be able to engage them without it.

Second, relatively speaking, the competitive advantage conferred by sales effectiveness has just begun to emerge. It may well retain its power to win sales for ten or fifteen years or longer, depending on how many salespeople recognize and strive to attain it, before it becomes a commonplace standard and an expectation in the customer's eyes.

So, the bad news is that the same evolutionary pattern that brought the sales professional to the top spot in the customer's buying decision will eventually create the same kind of competition that transformed price, quality, and features from substantial differentiation factors into entry fees. At some point in the future, customers will expect sales professionalism as a matter of course. When that happens, some other factor, perhaps one that has not even appeared on our radar as yet, will emerge as the leading competitive advantage.

Here's the good news, though. Given the current level of professionalism in sales, we expect that those rare salespeople who are already meeting their customers' expectations and demands, and those who can quickly respond to them, will enjoy a good long run at the peak of their profession.

The Demand for Sales Effectiveness

Before we set off pell-mell on a quest for sales effectiveness, it only makes sense to examine why it has come to occupy such a commanding position in your customers' minds. Why do customers say that the person selling them products and services is more influential than price or quality or the seller's ability to provide total solutions (which are the three influencers most often cited, after sales effectiveness)?

We've already touched on one major reason: the competition among vendors in these other areas is in the process of reducing those areas to table stakes. Chances are very good that your major competitors are offering similar levels of quality, that their prices are roughly equal to yours, and that, like you, they are positioning their offerings as solutions. If your customers don't see any significant differences between the price, quality, and solutions offered by you and your competitors, these attributes will have little impact on their buying decisions.

Granted, your company will almost always have some unique advantages to offer customers, even if they are only marketing-based advantages, such as brand or reputation. Perhaps you also offer greater ease of installation or a more comprehensive service plan or a newly developed product feature that is not available from your competitors—yet. The problem with these advantages is that as they prove capable of attracting a substantial number of customers, your competitors will quickly undertake to meet and exceed them. Consider what happens to the sales of prescription drugs on the day that their patent protection expires. Your neighborhood pharmacy has generic versions already stocked and ready to sell the minute it is legally allowed to sell them, and the revenues produced by the original drug plummet. IMS Health calculated that the expiration of prescription drug patents in 2006 alone would result in the loss of $23 billion in revenue to pharmaceutical firms worldwide.[1]

When there are fewer or no legal protections, competitors can catch up as quickly as they choose. A recent *New York Times* story that detailed the spread of luxury bedding within the hotel industry provides a good example.[2] In 1999, Westin Hotels and Resorts pioneered this innovation within the large hotel chains when it introduced the "Heavenly Bed." In addition to attracting travelers with the promise of a "sleep experience," the concept became a new revenue generator as Westin began selling its branded bedding accessories. (In 2005, the revenue from the sales of these products hit $10 million.) Of course, the other major players took notice and "virtually every other hotel chain" upgraded its bedding, according to the *Times*. Hilton Hotels introduced the "Serenity Bed" and sells its accessories online. Marriott announced 300-thread-count sheets, feather beds, and so on. How do customers feel about this? Virtually everyone is happier with more comfortable bedding, but if every major hotel chain offers it, travelers needn't think about it much. They will get it whether they stay at a Westin or a Hilton or a Marriott. Of course, the same thing happens with your business products and services. Look at the proliferation of Customer Relationship Management (CRM) software and computer servers and outsourced call centers. As offerings proliferate and become more and more ubiquitous, the competitive advantages inherent in the quality, price, and sophistication of these products and services are reduced to standardized expectations. Thus, over time, they exert less and less influence on customers.

A second major reason why sales effectiveness has emerged as the most influential factor in customers' buying decisions is closely related to the battles that erupt whenever a company discovers a reproducible advantage. These battles among competing vendors tend to generate more choices for their customers. Sometimes, the more choices customers have, the more difficult it is for them to choose, and the less likely they are to buy. In his book *Future Shock*, Alvin Toffler called this phenomenon "overchoice." Professors John Gourville of Harvard Business School and Dilip Soman of University of Toronto's Rotman School of Management have been studying how overchoice impacts consumer brands. They discovered that the accepted wisdom that more variety means more market share is not always true. It all depends on how the choices offered by sellers are aligned within the overall product mix. There are many cases, particularly when there are multiple attributes that require the customer to make many tradeoff decisions (as in the feature choices on computers, for instance), when "an increasingly large assortment can negatively impact consumer choice and brand share."[3] In other words, you can offer your customers more features and benefits and win fewer sales!

Thus, when sellers get into innovation races, they can inadvertently make things even more confusing for customers. As new product features and technologies explode, sellers can easily outrun the customer's ability to comprehend their offerings. Think about the burgeoning choices in telecommunications. At this point in its evolution, how many business customers understand all of the implications, requirements, and costs of VoIP (Internet-based phone service)?

How do you, as a salesperson or a sales executive, overcome overchoice? One answer is by guiding the customer through the decision process. When technologies are emerging and choices are multiplying, customers develop a growing dependence on knowledgeable salespeople (their outsourced managers) to guide them through the maze of choices they suddenly face. In other words, salesperson effectiveness becomes a more and more influential factor in the customer's buying decision.

So, competitive advantages ultimately spawn races—the race for quality, the race for total solutions, the race to lower prices—that undermine both the differentiating power of those advantages and the ability of customers to understand the myriad alternatives. These races support and promote the customer's demand for sales effectiveness. The fact that other competitive factors are more or less equal gives the professionalism of the salesperson greater weight in the customer's mind. The fact that the races often lead to increasingly sophisticated offerings creates greater customer dependence on sales professionals.

Of course, because sales effectiveness is a competitive advantage, it is also subject to these same forces. If that's the case, however, why has the demand risen and remained so high? The quick answer: the dramatic scarcity of highly effective salespeople.

The Supply Side of Sales Effectiveness

Millions of salespeople are working in business-to-business markets. But when we analyze customers' actual purchase decisions and correlate those decisions against carefully collected ratings of the various and competing salespeople they deal with, we find that there are far fewer salespeople whom they consider world-class professionals. Over the past fourteen years, we have interviewed 80,000 business customers and collected data on 7,200 sales forces representing more than fifteen major industries. In the period between 1992 and 2002, business customers identified fewer than twenty of these sales organizations as world-class. In other words, they have awarded world-class status to less than three-tenths of one percent of the sales forces that they rated. (We should also note that these organizations sometimes represent only a single business group or division within a corporation, not its entire sales force and, most importantly, that having won in a given year was no guarantee of maintaining that lofty accomplishment. In fact, four of the companies lost world-class status after being acquired by or having merged with another company.)

Customer-Selected World-Class Sales Forces (1993–2002)

Allegiance Healthcare Corporation

Applied Industrial Technologies

AT&T Consumer Products

AT&T Middle Market

Boise Cascade Office Products (twice)

Corporate Express

CPW Computer Centers

Dupont

Exxon Chemical

GE Industrial Control Systems

Global Imaging Systems

Grainger, Inc.

Honda Motor Company

IBM Corporation

Insight Enterprises

John Deere & Company

Moore Corporation

Motion Industries (twice)

There are good reasons why highly effective salespeople are so hard to find:

First, senior leadership isn't focused on the sales effectiveness advantage. The commitment of senior leadership is the one requirement on which all corporate strategies and programs depend; by and large, however, the senior leaders of business-to-business sellers tend to be more focused on the sales numbers than on the capabilities of their sales forces. Many leaders, particularly in manufacturing sectors, don't even think of the process of getting their products into customers' hands as a sales process. They think of this work as "distribution." They talk about their sales forces—when they have sales forces—as one of several distribution channels.

One reason for this lack of focus is that most CEOs haven't spent significant amounts of time as salespeople or sales managers. Most of them have rotated through sales in short stints, usually early in their careers and in lower-echelon roles, on their way to the top of the corporate ladder. But, with a handful of notable exceptions (such as Hewlett-Packard CEO Mark Hurd and Lou Gerstner's successor at IBM, Sam Palmisano), few have had substantial experience running sales organizations. As a result, corporate leaders tend to think of sales as what Jeff Thull, president of Prime Resource Group, so aptly calls a "black box." He describes it like this:

> *The black box view of sales is an attitude that we frequently find among senior executives who do not have sales experience. To them, the workings of the sales department are largely a mystery. They can set goals and send them into the black box of the sales force, and they can tell whether the goals have been reached—after the fact. But they can't effectively manage what happens between the two points.*[4]

Compounding the problem is that there are also many other compelling issues competing for the attention of senior executives, not the least of which is the fulfillment of their corporate mission statements and strategies. Many leaders are aggressively pursuing promises to create total solutions for their customers or provide the highest quality product or the most competitive price. But the pursuit of mission statements that declare "We will have the most professional sales force in our industry" is far less common.

Further, sales effectiveness is typically not seen as a competitive advantage that is worthy of undivided attention in the

CEO's suite. Rather, the sales function is usually defined as a subprocess of marketing. When sales results meet or exceed their targets, the credit tends to go to the current strategic focus: "We successfully brought a total solution to market" or "Our drive for greater productivity allowed us to price more aggressively." When the results fall short, however, it tends to get blamed on the sales department. As in, "We've got to get some new sales leadership in place and shake things up a little." It appears that most senior leaders do not realize that the fact that they are competing on low-differentiation influencers—such as price, quality, or the comprehensiveness of their solutions—rather than on sales effectiveness may be what is leading them to diminishing returns in the first place.

Second, most employer-sponsored sales training isn't designed to deliver the* right *skills and behaviors. This is not to say that companies do not invest significant resources in the effort to create and develop their sales forces. They do. In fact, *Training* magazine's annual U.S. Training Industry Study found that companies budgeted $51.1 billion for employee training in 2005, and 52.4 percent of the companies surveyed report that they invest what is clearly a significant portion of those funds in sales training.[5] However, when we consider the outcomes that the typical salesperson training is designed to produce, a fundamental disconnect quickly becomes apparent.

The most common forms of sales training are *self-improvement programming*, which is aimed at building the salesperson's personal productivity, enthusiasm, and energy, and *sales process training*, which teaches salespeople to prospect, cold call, present, overcome objections, close, and so on. Do these types of training enhance the effectiveness of salespeople? From the seller's perspective, they certainly do. Salespeople who can't manage their time or muster the energy to pick up the phone or who don't know how to close surely aren't going to be able to maximize their results. Although these two layers of training are important, they nevertheless are typically the only training that salespeople receive, and that leaves an important part of the story untold.

If we consider the desired outcomes of sales training from the customer's perspective, the training curriculum looks much less than complete. Customers don't really care whether a salesperson is eager to hit the phones in the morning, or how adept a salesperson is at setting appointments or delivering presentations. In fact, most of the skills that do matter to customers, as we'll see in coming chapters, are left largely unaddressed in most sales training. Buyers obviously have a different set of needs than do sellers, and they want salespeople who are trained to meet those needs. If their needs aren't met, they don't complain about sales training; they simply refuse to buy at all, or they buy from a competitor. When sales training does address the customers' needs, it usually only happens because their needs happen to align with those of the seller. By and large, sales training does not enhance sales effectiveness *as defined by customers.*

Another reason that sales training often neglects the customer is that there is no widely accepted, well-established body of knowledge for the discipline of sales. The quality revolution, which initially focused the attention of our nation's companies on a customer-first orientation, virtually bypassed sales organizations. TQM was not applied to sales, and there is no ISO certification for sales, nor has Six Sigma been applied to the sales function in any significant way.

Finally, even when sales training is not misdirected, the results it produces can be problematic. Some studies suggest that as little as 15 percent of employer-provided training "sticks" in the employee's mind. All of this might be less serious if our colleges and universities were graduating future salespeople who were properly prepared for the day when they will enter the professional world, but as we will explain in the next point, our educational institutions also have a hand in the scarcity of sales effectiveness.

Third, far too few salespeople are prepared for their careers prior to entering the work world. As mentioned earlier, senior leaders often do not see their sales forces as a source of competitive advantage. One major reason for this is that their formal educations did not teach them to view the sales function in this light. At the time most of the leaders of our major corporations earned their undergraduate and graduate degrees, the colleges and universities they attended did not have well-developed sales curricula.

Surprisingly, the vast majority of the nation's colleges and universities still do not consider the discipline of sales and selling as professional pursuits. (In academic circles, a profession is defined as a body of knowledge that has specialties, one or more "certifiable" or "licensable" bodies of expertise, and an accrediting process.) Instead, most institutions of higher learning offer a smattering of sales courses, such as Introduction to Sales and Sales Management, which are mainly attended by their marketing majors. Even these basic courses are often relatively recent additions to the catalogs of business schools. For example, Baylor University now has a nationally known sales curriculum, but it wasn't until the late 1980s and early 1990s (according to Dr. Jeff Tanner of Baylor's Hankamer School of Business) that sales courses began appearing there.

Formal academic certificate and degree programs in professional selling are very rare, and those that do exist are still in early developmental stages compared to other business specialties. The Sales Centre at Ohio University established one of the first certification programs for sales in 1997. It awards a Sales Certificate that is recognized on the university transcript after the successful completion of a 28-credit hour curriculum that includes a 300-hour internship.[6] One of the first institutions to offer a bachelor of business administration in professional selling was Baylor's Hankamer School of Business, and it only awarded its first degree in that major in 2003. The world's first bachelor of science degree in professional sales didn't appear until April

2005, when William Paterson University announced it had established that degree track. Although it's true that sales programs are starting to sprout up in the nation's colleges and universities, as of this writing, only 35 of the nation's 4,158 colleges and universities offer degree programs in professional selling.

The very limited number of degree programs in professional selling stands in sharp contrast to the numbers of students who finish their schooling and enter the sales profession. Here's a statistic that surprises everyone who hears it: *Two-thirds of college graduates now take sales jobs upon the completion of their formal education.* It's actually not so surprising, when you think about it. Sales jobs have long been a common entry point to the corporate world for students with liberal arts degrees in disciplines such as English, art, history, and other nonbusiness areas. Students with business degrees, who often earn spots in the management trainee programs of major corporations, often find themselves starting in sales too.

So, we have roughly 66 percent of college and university graduates entering sales jobs, and 0.8 percent of colleges and universities preparing them for those jobs. It's obvious that the demand for sales effectiveness is not being met in the academic world.

Further, the opinions given by expert sources at places like the Sales Centre at Ohio University suggest that the numbers of graduates entering sales is going to rise. The continued and often accelerating offshoring of business functions and processes is narrowing the job choices of America's graduates. It isn't just blue-collar jobs that we're losing. Related managerial positions in operations such as manufacturing and warehousing and distribution are migrating along with those functions.

Many other white-collar jobs are moving overseas too, and not just in the widely recognized sectors of software development, customer service, and call-center operations. Journalism jobs are being offshored; for example, in August 2004, Reuters Group PLC, the global business information giant, announced that it would cut costs by eliminating twenty editorial positions in the United States and Europe and hiring up to sixty replacements in India.[7] That same year, *Business 2.0* conducted a much-publicized experiment when it offshored the writing and production of a full section of the magazine. Legal services are being offshored, too. The *Wall Street Journal* recently reported that DuPont uses lawyers in India to help draft its patent applications; DirectoryM, an online marketing firm, offshored legal research to India. Forrester Research calculated that 29,000 legal jobs would be outsourced, mainly to India, by 2008.[8]

This is not a harangue against offshoring. That is an economic trend that is driven by globalization, and it is simply one of the realities of free market economies. Rather, it is evidence to support the increasing proportion of sales jobs in our economy as a whole. As other professions are offshored, the sales job category will grow in relative size and importance. These jobs will account for a larger percentage of our overall work force. Retail sales and, more important for our purposes in this book, face-to-face professional sales, usually won't lend themselves to outsourcing overseas. They both require immediacy and real-time interaction. Further, sellers will be loath to outsource a function that will increasingly be seen as a core competency. That translates into both a continuing shortage and an ever-growing demand for sales effectiveness.

Bridging the Sales Effectiveness Gap

Demand is high, supply is low, and the outlook is more of the same. The result is a gap, a Sales Effectiveness Gap, which stands between the customer's needs and the current skill level of salespeople. By the way, this gap may also help explain why such a great percentage of new salespeople are insufficiently prepared, fail to produce adequate results, and quickly leave (or lose) their positions.

Now, let's begin to focus on the opportunity instead of the problem. Customers tell us that they want to buy, and that they *do* buy, from highly effective sales professionals. We know that they consider very few salespeople to be "world-class professionals," so it's clear that whatever skills and capabilities we've been teaching salespeople in the past aren't fulfilling their customers' needs. So, a valuable opportunity exists for sales professionals who can capture the competitive advantage of sales effectiveness.

The first key to bridging the Sales Effectiveness Gap and capturing that advantage is defining what sales effectiveness means to *customers*. It is the customer's definition of sales excellence that is of primary importance in the quest for superior sales results. The importance of a customer-first focus probably doesn't come as a big surprise to you, but despite all the talk about it, true customer focus remains a critical input that is often overlooked when sales expertise is being considered. Just look at the bias toward sales process and personal productivity in most sales training, and the bias toward solutions in the materials and presentations that salespeople give to customers. (They almost always devote surprisingly little attention to the customer.) The result is that in the typical sale there is too much emphasis on the seller and the seller's solutions, and too little on the customer and the customer's requirements.

The larger goal of our Customer-Selected World-Class Sales Excellence studies has been to illuminate the customer side of the sales equation. We've now spent thirteen years surveying business-to-business customers in order to learn (a) what goals they expect sales professionals to help them accomplish in their businesses, and (b) which sales skills actually provide benefit in the pursuit of those goals. The answers that customers have given us, along with the correlation of that information to the actual purchasing behavior of those customers and the benchmarking of the sales forces that they defined as world-class, now enable us to confidently propose the answers to those two questions. As we've said, our purpose in this book is to use these findings to help you capture the competitive advantage of sales effectiveness, and to use that advantage to become a world-class sales professional.

In the next chapter, we will step into the business-to-business customer's world and try to answer the question, "What goals do customers expect you to help them accomplish?" We will identify and explore the three major customer demands and trends that are driving the business-to-business sales environment. Then, in the seven chapters of Part Two and Part Three, we will answer the second question: "What skills must you bring to the sale in order to satisfy your customers' demands?" These chapters will detail the customer rules and the roles you must be able to assume to fulfill them.

CHAPTER 2

What Your Customers Want

If you are a business-to-business salesperson, the most obvious measure of your effectiveness is the volume and the quality of business you earn from your customers. Your job is to engage customers, sell them products and services that can deliver the business results they desire, and ensure they receive those results so that they will allow you to repeat the process. At the end of predetermined time periods—each day, week, month, quarter, and/or year—the business you write is tallied, and your employer rewards you accordingly.

Many people are attracted to sales careers because they like working in a job where their performance and their rewards are so tangibly connected. They like the fact that their compensation, in addition to being potentially unlimited, is driven by their results. But what is the source of their sales results?

The only *direct source* of sales success is the customer's decision to buy. If enough customers decide to buy from you and they buy often enough, you make a significant contribution to your company's revenue growth, meet and exceed your sales quotas and targets, and earn your salary, commissions, and bonuses. If customers do not decide to buy from you (and that result occurs too frequently), negative and opposite reactions begin to occur. In a more direct manner than in most other business careers, your success as a salesperson is in the hands of your customers.

Everything else that we identify with sales excellence is actually an *indirect source* of success. The offering price, the features of the offering, the value that the offering delivers, and especially, the skills and behaviors of the salesperson are all aimed at influencing the customer's decision to buy. These attributes do not create sales success in and of themselves. However, when they cause the customer to act as intended, they result in a decision to buy, which in turn creates sales success.

This should sound like common sense to you (and rightly so), but too often, this causal chain gets abbreviated. Many sales experts, for instance, use a sort of shorthand: they tell us that a certain process or technique or mindset will create sales success, rather than saying that it will influence the customer's decision to buy, which in turn will create sales success. This is more than an exercise in semantics. The problem with abbreviating the causal chain in this way is that the customer—and the customer's direct role in your success—drops out of the equation.

Does Your Customer Come First?

Anything that causes us to lose sight of the primary role that customers play in sales success is dangerous. The danger increases when sales success starts to appear to be directly attributable to something other than customers, and "what customers want" becomes a secondary, or even worse, an inconsequential source of success.

By now, it's hard to believe that customers don't always come first in the minds of salespeople and their employers. The primacy of customers in business has been accepted for decades, and not just in sales alone. In 1954, more than a half century ago now, Peter Drucker clearly articulated the customer's role in business in his seminal book *The Practice of Management*. After declaring that the "only valid definition of business purpose" is "to create a customer," Drucker goes on to say:

> *It is the customer who determines what a business is. For it is the customer, and he alone, who through being willing to pay for a good or for a service, converts economic resources into wealth, things into goods. What the business thinks it produces is not of first importance—especially not to the future of the business and its success. What a customer thinks he is buying, what he considers "value," is decisive—it determines what a business is, what it produces and whether it will prosper.*[9]

As a result of Drucker's precepts, as well as those of many other management experts, the logical insistence that all businesses are first and foremost customer-driven has elevated customer focus to one of the most often heard corporate rallying cries. Business-to-business sellers are constantly proclaiming that they are "close to the customer" and, most recently, "customer-centric." Nevertheless, customer-centricity is fervently advocated far more often than it is effectively achieved. Here are three reasons why.

Reason #1: Strategic Disconnects

The long-term corporate strategies of sellers often cause them to become disconnected from their customers. Companies tend to define themselves in terms of a "driving force." In the 1970s, Benjamin Tregoe, the cofounder of the consulting firm Kepner-Tregoe, Inc., introduced the idea that there was one and only one driving force that should be the primary determinant of a company's strategy. Tregoe said that there were nine (later reduced to eight) possible driving forces a company could choose among. Only one of them, "market needs," was explicitly customer-focused.[10] Over the years, many other consultants and academicians adopted and adapted the driving-force concept. The problem with it, as with sales strategies and techniques, is that it is easy to slip into the mistake of thinking that your company's driving force, rather than the patronage of its customers, is the source of its success.

The farther your company's driving force is from the customer, the more common this problem becomes. Companies that are "return-driven" and define success by shareholder value often run afoul of their customers in the quest for short-term profit maximization. In a particularly egregious example, between 1998 and 2001, a handful of energy companies, including Enron, artificially inflated electricity prices in California, thereby causing the people of the state to pay $6.2 billion in overcharges.[11] Clearly, this is a serious perversion of the idea of customer focus.

"Production-driven" companies can also devalue the customer in the quest to maximize efficiency and output. Henry Ford's wildly popular Model T was originally available in five body colors. By 1914, Ford had eliminated all but one, giving rise to his apocryphal quote: "You can have it in any color you want, as long as it's black." The reduction in color alternatives reduced the time needed to finish a car from two weeks to just a day and a half. But Ford's myopic unwillingness to provide the options that customers wanted also led to the rise of his greatest competitor, General Motors. GM offered a wide variety of models and options, and rose to dominate the auto industry for the rest of the twentieth century.[12]

"Technology-driven" companies also fall prey to the "build it and they will come" mentality. They have been known to leave their customers behind in the pursuit of innovation and increasingly sophisticated products. In fact, this is such a common occurrence that Harvard Business School's Clayton Christensen, who has studied the effect of innovation on corporate and industry performance, has given it a name: "performance oversupply."[13]

Reason #2: Short-Term Goal Conflicts

Often, the customer does not come first because salespeople and their companies have short-term goals that conflict with the customer's best interests. All salespeople have personal goals. For instance, they work hard to fulfill their quotas and hit sales targets. They rightly want to maximize their personal income and earn bonuses.

Salespeople also have goals that are imposed on them by their employers. Their companies make them responsible for bolstering revenues, especially as the end of reporting periods loom. They are expected to sell excess inventory, as well as meet the sales targets for newly developed products and services.

These goals are neither improper nor unethical in and of themselves; they all are legitimate sales goals. At the same time, however, we should recognize that none of them are customer-focused goals. A salesperson's personal success and/or a vendor's corporate success do not provide a direct benefit to the customer. In fact, there are many occasions, such as when a vendor charges one customer a higher price than another for a product, or a salesperson encourages a customer to buy a product even though it is not the best alternative, when the short-term success of a vendor or a salesperson is antithetical to the customer's success.

Reason #3: Customer Data Shortfalls

Finally, sellers fail to put customers first because they simply do not know what their customers want, expect, and hope to achieve. Nor, by and large, do they know the costs and the value associated with their relationships with their customers.

"Customer satisfaction" is the metric that most often features prominently on CEO scorecards, in employee incentive programs, and in advertising and other marketing campaigns. Most companies use customer satisfaction surveys to determine how well they are serving their customers. But, as Fred Reichheld, director emeritus at Bain & Co., refreshingly declares, "[S]atisfaction surveys are a joke." He lists ten reasons why this is so, including that most are poorly constructed, not validated against customer behavior, subject to manipulation, and not actionable.[14]

In fact, most sellers, whom we would expect to exaggerate their own levels of customer knowledge, admit that they are not close to their customers. In 2005, an annual study of business executives conducted by the Strativity Group, Inc., found that:

- 58 percent of executives said that their company "does not conduct true dialogue with customers."
- 66.8 percent of executives said that they "don't meet frequently with customers."
- 59 percent said that the role of the customer was "not well-defined" at their companies.
- 54 percent said that their company "does not deserve customer loyalty."

Strativity also found that the majority of the executives surveyed *did not know* the cost of customer complaint (90.3 percent), the cost of complaint resolution (90 percent), their annual customer retention rate (73.8 percent), the annual value of a customer (87.1 percent), or the cost of acquiring a new customer (91.4 percent). The firm's hard-to-fault conclusion: "Companies remained self-centric, transaction-based and product-focused."[15]

The Hierarchy of Customer Wants

While the barriers to putting customers first can appear daunting, salespeople have no choice but to overcome them. To become truly effective as a salesperson and win favorable customer decisions, your strategic focus must be customer-driven. After all, no matter what drives you and your company, it is the customer's decision to buy that drives sales and corporate success.

This also means that the customer's best interests come before your personal goals and your company's goals. This voluntary, but nevertheless rigorous, commitment to the customer's best interests is one of the integral components of a *profession*. All professionals in the formal sense of the word—doctors, lawyers, accountants, and so on—are expected to adopt and exhibit this characteristic (and are censured if they do not). If sales is to become a profession, salespeople must make the same commitment.

In order to become a customer-centric salesperson, you first must see the world from your customer's perspective. You need to know what your customers are hoping to accomplish as well as why your customers are looking to you for help. This knowledge provides the foundation that defines and supports the roles, behaviors, and skills you need to master to become an effective salesperson. The specific details of customer knowledge will, of course, vary by the individual customer and industry. But in generic terms, all of the answers that the business customers we've surveyed over the past fourteen years have given us follow one of three common themes. These themes fit into a *hierarchy of wants* that encompasses what business customers look to salespeople and vendors to provide.

The hierarchy of customer wants is like a pyramid with three ascending levels. The base of the pyramid is the fundamental want that underlies everything customers seek from sellers: *the demand for substantiated value.* Businesses seek a return on every investment they make, and to be of value, these returns must be tangible as well as measurable in financial terms. The second customer want resides in the middle of the pyramid, supported by the demand for value: *the demand for solutions.* Customers do not relate to value—cost savings and/or increased revenues—in terms of products and services. Instead, they think in terms of solutions and how those solutions enable them to resolve problems and/or capture opportunities. At the peak of the pyramid is the third customer want: *the demand for outsourcing.* Outsourcing is the most sophisticated expression of the customer desire for solutions. It requires that vendors actually take ownership of, execute, and manage a portion of the customer's business.

The Hierarchy of Customer Wants

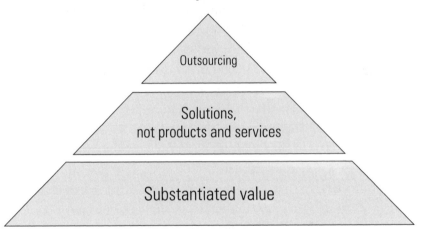

Want #1: "We Want Substantiated Value"

Your corporate customers express success in financial terms, such as revenues, net income, operating expenses, and net earnings. They must be able to judge the value of the products and services you are trying to sell them in those same terms. Further, they do not want anecdotal proof of value, such as case studies of your existing customers. Nor do they want generic proof of value, such as studies that compare the performance of your existing customers against industry averages. They want a customized, quantified return on investment (ROI), and more often than ever before, they want you to guarantee that they will attain the ROI specified. They want substantiated value.

The customer demand for substantiated value is being driven by two growth trajectories. First, it is growing as the products and services you are offering your customers become more sophisticated, and the impact of your offerings on your customers' businesses becomes more difficult for customers to understand on their own. Second, it is growing because of economic conditions. Corporate spending has been reduced and increasingly more carefully scrutinized since the evaporation of the "irrational exuberance" that drove corporate performance at the turn of the century. Since 2000, both of these trajectories have joined to create a nearly unanimous customer demand for proven, tangible value in business-to-business transactions.

The evidence of this demand is clear among buyers of information technology (IT), which remains one of the largest and most diverse of the business-to-business markets. In 2002, the year after the meltdown of the dot-coms (as well as many of the IT vendors that were depending on them for continued high growth), Ernst and Young surveyed Fortune 1000 IT buyers and found that 79 percent of them considered "financial justification" an important part of their purchasing decisions. Eight out of ten IT buyers also expected vendors to provide that financial justification. Interestingly, however, these findings stand in stark contrast to how well IT buyers believe that vendors fulfill the demand for substantiated value. In the same Ernst and Young survey, only 2 percent of IT buyers said that vendors were exceeding their expectations in communicating financial value. Further, only 2 percent said they trusted vendor-supplied metrics.[16]

This is not an isolated case of customer skepticism. In 2003, *Network World* invited its readers to participate in an ad hoc survey about ROI calculators—the software programs that many sellers have adopted to help estimate the value of their solutions for customers. It found that customer trust in vendor ROI calculators *decreases* the higher up the corporate ladder that the customer resides. One-third of low-level managers said that they did not trust the calculators, but 87 percent of mid-level managers and 100 percent of executives said they did not trust them.[17] Clearly the ability to provide credible ROI estimates represents a major opportunity for business-to-business salespeople.

This all points to the fact that there is rarely alignment in the way salespeople are engaging business customers and the way that customers want to be engaged. Craig Wilson, director of corporate marketing at International Paper, described the two camps very well during a global survey of senior sales executives we conducted in 2002. "There is a difference between selling and value managing," he said. "Selling is about what you want the customers to hear about your product and your features. Value managing is understanding what the customer needs, providing the benefits the customer is looking for, and having the customer understand how those benefits translate into either a better top line or a better bottom line."

One major cause for the misalignment is the fact that substantiating the financial metrics of products and services for customers is no simple matter. When your products and services have multiple impacts within the customer's organization, metrics can be hard to identify and measure. Credible value calculations can require a high degree of access as well as a substantial investment in time that salespeople and/or customers are often unwilling to undertake. Sometimes, the levels of return that customers expect are unrealistic. In a 2005 *InformationWeek* poll, 53 percent of buyers said that they require a 100 percent return on their IT investments within the first year![18] It is obviously impossible to meet such a demand if you sell enterprise resource planning (ERP) software or radio frequency identification (RFID) solutions that can take years to fully implement. Sometimes, the levels of return that salespeople promise are unrealistic, too. That's one good reason vendor-supplied ROI figures are less than credible to so many buyers.

These difficulties notwithstanding, the first of the three "wants" of business customers is clear and, increasingly, not open to negotiation. Corporate buyers are demanding that their suppliers prove their sales promises by demonstrating, delivering, and quantifying the value of the solutions they purchase. They want to be able to evaluate their vendors in the same way they evaluate their internal operations. They want measurable results and they want vendors whom they can hold accountable for those results.

Want #2: "We Want Solutions, Not Products and Services"

Your corporate customers are not the least bit interested in buying your products and services. They *are* interested in operating as efficiently as possible, in fulfilling the needs and demands of their own customers to the best of their ability, and in meeting their corporate growth and financial targets. Your customers' desire for your products and services extends only as far as those products and services can help fulfill these goals. This is the reality that lies behind the second "want" that business customers have articulated in our surveys: the demand for solutions.

Some observers see the customer demand for solutions as one that has only recently emerged, but this is not a new phenomenon. Business customers have never been interested in buying products and services. They always made purchases in order to solve problems and capture opportunities. Their interest in solutions, however, is often obscured by their behavior and by the accepted sales wisdom that developed around it.

Take a copy machine, for instance. When the toner cartridge is depleted, the customer buys a new one. He buys it based on product attributes—availability, life of the product, price, and quality. But he actually wants copies, not toner. He knows he cannot get the copies he needs without it. Since the customer already knows that a toner cartridge is the right solution to the problem, you can focus solely on its attributes and win the sale.

But what happens when the solution is not so evident? Say the customer is opening a new office and needs to properly equip it. He could buy a copier or a scanner or an all-in-one printer. He could buy a high-output machine that will be shared on a network or provide smaller machines on each desktop. He could buy outright or finance or lease. All of these alternatives add complexity to the customer's decision. Unless he is an expert on document handling, he probably does not understand the many different solutions available or even the different kinds of document services his office will require. If you call on this customer and attempt to sell him a copier based on its attributes, you are not addressing any of these issues, and therefore are unlikely to win the sale.

In addition to the complexities that arise when the customer's problem is difficult to clearly define, buying decisions also become harder as solutions become more sophisticated. Technology is always advancing, and the number of options that sellers offer customers tends to grow over time. The more choice the customer has, the more difficult the buying decision. Buying decisions also become harder as customer constraints increase. Business customers, especially senior executives, have greater spans of responsibility than ever before. They have less and less time to make more and more decisions, often on issues with which they are not fully conversant. They do not have the time or expertise needed to immerse themselves in the details of your products and services. They need to think in terms of solving problems and/or capturing opportunities. In these situations, customers want salespeople who think along these same lines, rather than in terms of features and benefits. They look to salespeople as consultants and advisors who can guide them through the maze of alternatives to the best solution.

By and large, business-to-business salespeople and their managers are well aware of the demand for solutions. In our 2002 Business Challenges survey, we interviewed more than ninety senior sales executives from business-to-business sellers located around the world. We asked them, "How will salespeople have to change or develop in the future in order to help drive company growth?" The answer given three times more often than any other, by more than 60 percent of the executives, was "more competence 'consulting.'" They want to develop sales forces that are able to sell solutions. They want salespeople who are experts at sales strategies such as consultative selling and solution selling.

"The sales professional will have to become more competent in the issues that our customers are grappling with," Jack Luker, VP of Sales at Xpedx, explained to us. "Customers are demanding solution-based value propositions that bring measurable value to their bottom line. Product features and benefits are still important, but the thrust of our propositions today must be based on a more elaborate set of value drivers. The ability of the sales professional to rise to this expectation can be a key differentiator."

The recognition of the customer's demand for solutions and the desire to create sales forces that can sell solutions continues to spread through the business-to-business arena. In May 2005, Deloitte Consulting LLP hosted a forum attended by senior sales executives from more than thirty of the world's largest companies. Deloitte surveyed the attendees and reported that "100 percent said their companies were highly committed to selling solutions—not just products."[19]

The fact that every attendee at the Deloitte forum was pursuing solution-based sales strategies is certainly indicative of the customer demand. But even more interesting is the fact that 48 percent of the executives also admitted that they had not yet achieved the returns they expected from solution selling. Only 15 percent responded, "Yes, very much so," when asked if they had achieved their expected returns. Recognizing the customer demand for solutions and actually fulfilling that demand have turned out to be two very different things. It is also a gap we hope to help you bridge in the coming chapters.

Basically, your customers want to partner with suppliers who demonstrate a comprehensive understanding of their business and who are capable of solving their problems. Selling discrete products and services isn't enough to fulfill this demand. Instead, your customers are searching for vendors who can apply, implement, and manage solutions to their problems. Major business-to-business sellers already recognize this customer need, but as yet, most have not yet been able to fully satisfy it.

Want #3: "We Want to Outsource Everything Except Our Core Competencies"

Your corporate customers are in the midst of the largest jettisoning of business processes in history, and they are searching for vendors they can trust to execute a wide variety of activities ranging from accounts payable to research and development. These customers are following the lead of highly successful companies such as Beaverton, Oregon–based Nike, Inc., the world's leading shoemaker, which garnered widespread attention as an outsourcing pioneer.

Nike does not manufacture any of its footwear. Instead, it invests its time and resources in product design and development, and marketing and sales. It contracts with other companies to manufacture its many products, a strategy that allows the company to avoid huge investments in plants, equipment, operational management, workers, and so on. As of May 31, 2004, Nike's outsourced manufacturing included 830 contract factories employing more than 624,631 contract workers globally.[20]

Nike's business model is one that more and more companies have adopted. It is powered by the concept of "core competencies," first introduced by professors Gary Hamel and C. K. Prahalad in a popular *Harvard Business Review* article and later expanded upon in their book *Competing for the Future*. Hamel and Prahalad suggested that every company had numerous competencies, which they defined as bundles of skills and technologies. But, they went on to theorize, the key to business success was a Nike-like focus on "those competencies that lie at the center, rather than the periphery, of long-term competitive advantage."[21] In other words, the focus needs to be on only those core competencies capable of creating customer value leverage, distinctive differentiation in the marketplace, and an array of opportunities for the future.

If your customers believe the key to success is focusing all of their efforts and resources on core competencies, what does that mean for all of the other activities they conduct in the process of doing business? Rather than leave those activities starved for attention and hobbled, the logical answer is to outsource them to vendors who see them as core competencies. Thus, the race to capture leadership in the arenas defined by core competencies has also helped create and accelerate the customer demand for outsourcing non-core activities.

Your customers are able to fulfill this demand with ever-increasing ease. Advances in information technology have created bridges over geographic boundaries, both enabling and encouraging the outsourcing demand. The digital revolution and global networks allow customers to send their processes, and obtain the products and services needed to execute them, anywhere in the world.

The lowering of ideological and political boundaries has also provided your customers with innumerable new outsourcing opportunities. Harvard University's Richard B. Freeman, Asherman Professor of Economics, studies the impact of what he calls "The Great Doubling." Freeman is referring to the literal doubling of the global work force—to 2.93 billion workers—that has occurred since 1990 as India, China, and the nations of the former Soviet bloc have joined the global economy.[22] A notable result of this huge increase in the supply of both skilled and unskilled labor has been the corporate drive to capture the savings inherent in this glut of labor. The offshoring of a broad diversity of jobs, which we described in the previous chapter, is one consequence of this reality. The offshoring of outsourcing services and business processes is another.

The evidence of the growing customer demand for outsourcing is all around us. The exact size of the global outsourcing market is hard to nail down, but current estimates start at around $300 billion annually. Executives at the research firm Gartner, Inc., report that by 2008, services outsourcing, which is the newest and fastest-growing segment of the market, will reach $750 billion.[23]

More evidence can be seen in the rush of companies to service the fast-growing demand for outsourcing. IBM's success over the past decade has been driven by its recognition of and adjustment to this trend. Its much-heralded return to profitability under the leadership of Lou Gerstner was driven by a switch from a product orientation to a service orientation. Now, under Sam Palmisano's leadership, the company has left its equipment roots even farther behind, selling off its PC business to Chinese computer maker Lenovo and continuing the shift from services to outsourcing. In 2005, IBM reported that the revenues from its Strategic Outsourcing business, its IT outsourcing arm, reached $19.7 billion, making it the world's leading outsourcing company by revenue.

Accenture, the consulting arm of the now-defunct accounting firm Arthur Andersen & Company, has also been transforming itself to fulfill the customer demand for outsourcing. In fiscal 2004 and 2005, outsourcing was the engine that drove growth at Accenture, providing $5 billion and $5.99 billion in revenue, respectively, according to its SEC filings. The consulting firm now provides a wide variety of outsourcing services: business process outsourcing in functions such as human resources, finance and accounting, and procurement; application outsourcing, such as the development and management of enterprise-level software programs including PeopleSoft, SAP, and Oracle; and infrastructure outsourcing, such as technical support, security, and network management.

These billions in outsourcing dollars all come from a single source: business customers who want to be able to focus on what they do best (whether it be development, production, distribution, sales, or service), lower their costs, and enhance their productivity. In this process of focusing, they are seeking to outsource everything that is not central to their business, and to do so constructively and at the most cost-effective price.

Translating Customer Wants into Sales Excellence

The three customer wants revealed during our Customer-Selected World Class Sales Excellence studies are more than a wish list. They are a mandate and a challenge to you. Your customers' hierarchy of wants drives their expectations and demands of vendors, and it should drive your company's responses, too. Most important for our purposes here, the fact that your customers want substantiated value in return for their investments, solutions rather than products and services, and the opportunity to outsource their non-core activities should also shape your approach to selling.

When we identified the three customer wants during our studies, we reached something of a defining moment ourselves. Now that we knew what customers wanted to accomplish, we were able to ask them the next logical question: "How do you want salespeople to support you in pursuit of your goals?"

Of course, in terms of generating results that are statistically valid, our job was not quite as simple as asking customers a single question. We needed to define and focus a series of questions. We had to ask them properly, as well as interpret and record answers. In addition, we had to determine the "share of wallet" that each respondent awarded each salesperson, and correlate their answers against the purchasing behavior.

This work entailed sorting and coding hundreds of thousands of responses of business customers into what turned out to be fifteen categories. Then, those categories were reduced to those that are directly applicable to salespeople, and within their control. Next, they were weighted to ensure that they were statistically significant, because there is no point in devoting time and effort to developing sales skills that are not capable of creating a substantial result. Ultimately, seven factors were revealed, factors that business-to-business customers believe define the world-class salesperson.

Factors predicting world-class sales status, 1993 versus 2000

1. Personally manages my satisfaction 59%
   38%
2. Understands our business 24%
   27%
3. Is a customer advocate 21%
   15%
4. Is knowledgeable of applications 19%
   25%
5. Is easily accessible 10%
   N/A
6. Solves our problems 9%
   13%
7. Is innovative in response to our needs 6%
   21%

Legend
2000
1993

The seven factors that business customers most often identified offer us two major insights: the behavioral *rules* that they expect salespeople to adhere to, and the corresponding professional *roles*, and the associated skills, that they expect salespeople to embody. These are the seven customer rules and the sales roles that support them:

Rule #1: "You must be personally accountable for our desired results." The best salespeople, and those to whom customers award the largest portion of their business, take personal responsibility for the customer's results. Of course, these salespeople neither do all of the work that is required themselves, nor are they directly employed by their customers. But they do act as the single point of contact for the customer and they ensure that customers buy the best solutions *and* achieve the value they expected. They act as business agents—that is, surrogate managers—who are responsible for every aspect of the relationship between the buyer and seller, especially the achievement of solution benefits.

Rule #2: "You must understand our business." This rule flows logically from the first: in order to personally manage a customer account, salespeople must understand the customer's business. This requires a deeper understanding than the qualification profile that most salespeople use to identify prospects. It means understanding how the customer's business works—its competencies and business strategies and organizational culture. It means understanding the customer's customer. It means seeing the customer's business as its CEO sees the business.

Rule #3: "You must be on our side." Although customers have little or no control over what happens to their purchases within the seller's company, the seller's internal processes, such as design, manufacturing, and logistics, can have a tremendous impact on the results they obtain. For this reason, customers expect salespeople to be their representatives within the seller's organization. The best salespeople ensure that the solutions that their customers have purchased move through their own companies as required and promised. When necessary, they manipulate their own company's systems to see that the customer is properly served. They also act as the voice of the customer, keeping their company informed of the needs and desires present in the marketplace. They are advocates and expediters, representing the best interests of the customer throughout the sales engagement and within the seller's organization.

Rule #4: "You must bring us applications." Customers want salespeople who think beyond features and benefits to applications. They want to know how to use products and services to achieve their goals, and they want to be sure the solutions they buy can be properly implemented in their unique environment. That's why the best salespeople act as consultants, assisting customers in their quest to capture the promised value of features and benefits through effective application.

Rule #5: "You must be easily accessible." Global *is* local in today's transnational, 24/7 business-to-business environment. This ongoing expansion of corporate boundaries has been accompanied by a corresponding growth in customer demand for local, accessible sales representation. Today's best salespeople are travelers who leap geographic, political, and cultural boundaries to instantly relieve customers' stress.

Rule #6: "You must solve our problems." In yesterday's sales world, the closing of the sale marked the end of the sales engagement and the salesperson's responsibilities. Today, the closing of the sale simply marks the end of the beginning. Customers expect salespeople to not only solve their problems during the transaction itself, but throughout the full term of the business relationship. The best salespeople act as troubleshooters who realize the inevitability of problems and, instead of hiding from them, commit to solving them quickly and effectively.

Rule #7: "You must be innovative in responding to our needs." Because change is the only constant in today's business-to-business environment, your customers expect you to respond with proactive and continuous innovation to their spoken and unspoken needs. To meet this demand, the best sales professionals are adopting the role of the innovator, acting as the point person in this effort and, as the closest customer contact, being the first to recognize and react to new business opportunities.

These are the rules and roles that represent your customers' definitions of world-class selling in business-to-business markets. They are also the quickest route to the only direct source of sales success—the customer's decision to buy. We will explore each of the rules in greater detail in the next seven chapters.

PART TWO

The Foundational Rules of Professional Competence

From a statistical point of view, when the criteria that predict an outcome are considered as a group, they must be weighted. This is because each influences the other criteria as well as the predicted outcome. When we apply the proper weighting factors to the seven skills that business customers say define world-class salespeople, we find that the first three skills have a disproportionately large influence on sales success. These three skills, which we call the foundational rules of professional competence, are the ones that are capable of lifting a salesperson above the vast majority of their colleagues and competitors in their customers' minds.

The most striking characteristic of the first three rules is that they bear no relation to standard sales skills, such as lead generation, cold calling, overcoming objections, and closing. Rather, they represent the first three sales competencies. The rules and the competencies are derived from and directly connected to the top three factors that actually predict which salespeople will win the initial business and the continuing, exceptional loyalty of their customers and thus, earn world-class sales status. Further, because the rules are customer-defined, they reflect the customer's goals in purchasing goods and services.

As we've seen, these goals are driven by the desire to outsource the acquisition of substantiated business value. Naturally, business customers expect the people who are selling them this outsourced value to ensure that they get it. The foundational rules and competencies make perfect sense when we see them from this perspective. Customers want to be able to depend on salespeople in the same way that they depend on any other manager in their companies. What do they expect of salespeople who act in the role of surrogate managers? To start, three things:

- First, your customers expect a salesperson who is accountable for managing the pieces of business they are outsourcing, someone who will not give excuses or get defensive, but will take responsibility for delivering the desired results.
- Second, your customers expect a salesperson who understands their businesses well enough that he or she can be trusted to provide sound advice, as well as make independent decisions that are properly aligned to their needs and goals.
- Third, your customers expect a salesperson who knows the politics, systems, processes, and procedures of his or her own company well enough to ensure that the results materialize as promised and planned.

What is in it for you if you provide these "managerial" services? Credibility and a competitive advantage that leads to an oversized share of the customer's wallet. No matter how effective salespeople are at executing their sales process, they cannot succeed without deserved business credibility. Without credibility, salespeople cannot convert leads into appointments, and potentially valuable new customer relationships are stillborn. Without credibility, customers will not provide the access and openness that salespeople need to properly execute today's consultative sales processes. Without credibility, customers will not buy the first time, nor in the future, because they will not trust in the salesperson's ability to deliver on promised solutions. Credibility is a key ingredient in successful selling. Demonstrating the three foundational competencies provides the basis for your credibility with customers.

CHAPTER 3

"You Must Be Personally Accountable for Our Desired Results"

Koans are paradoxical stories, statements, and questions that are used in the quest for spiritual enlightenment in Zen Buddhism. They can be quite cryptic, as in "What is the sound of one hand clapping?" Zen Buddhists believe that the process of thinking about koans can trigger important insights regarding their lives and the nature of the world. Here is a koan that can help you understand the first customer rule: "What sellers see as sales, their customers see as service."

How do the sellers' and the buyers' views differ? Well, if you are looking at sales from the sell side, it is about convincing customers to buy whatever it is that your company produces. The primary focus of your effort as a salesperson is the product (or service) you sell, and the value you bring to the customer is your knowledge of the product. You sell the product by finding a prospective customer, presenting the product's features and benefits, and asking the customer to purchase it. Your job is done when the deal is signed. This is a traditional, transaction-based sales paradigm. When you look at sales from the buy side, however, the view changes dramatically. Buyers see sales as a service function. The product they are buying is merely a means to a specific outcome or outcomes, a desired end. (This view corresponds perfectly with the customer's desire for solutions.) So, as a salesperson, your focus shifts from the product to the customer. Now, you need to consider and assist customers in recognizing their needs, analyze the various ways those needs can be satisfied, and oversee the fulfillment of those needs. All the product knowledge in the world will not tell you what a customer needs or wants to achieve. Product knowledge becomes only one aspect of the value you provide to the customer now. Further, your job is not done when you sell something. It is only done if and when you cannot assist the customer in realizing his or her desired outcomes any longer. This is a buy-side view of sales. It is a service-based paradigm.

Your customers' view of sales includes lots of added-value services that they expect salespeople to provide. Repeatedly, business customers tell us that they want to work with salespeople who are more oriented toward *service* (that is, managing the complete customer relationship) and *outcomes* (that is, making sure customers accomplish their intended goals). This demand for service and outcomes, according to the tens of thousands of business customers we've interviewed, lies at the heart of their primary expectation of salespeople and the first customer rule: *"You must be personally accountable for our desired results."*

Salespeople Are Business Agents

Management is the key concept at work in the first customer rule. The skill that business customers most frequently associate with world-class salespeople is their ability and willingness to act as surrogate managers.

On the surface, this seems like an odd expectation, and one that falls outside the scope of the typical description of a sales job. Customers do not employ salespeople as managers.

In fact, customers do not employ salespeople at all in the traditional sense of the word. Nor do their own employers usually think of salespeople as managers. Their job is to sell, not to manage. These are among the reasons so few salespeople actually see themselves as managers and why even fewer earn the

BUYERS AND SUPPLIERS

The labels we use to describe each other say a lot about how we see others and ourselves, too. In the case of sales, these labels illuminate the differences in how you and your customers view each other, as well as the relationship between you.

When sellers talk about customers in the generic sense, they often call them "buyers." What do buyers do? Obviously, they are expected to purchase whatever it is that the seller is offering. But there is not much meaning or relationship implied beyond that one-dimensional vision of an economic exchange. Interestingly, customers' purchasing departments are often staffed with "buyers." This should offer us a clue as to why purchasing professionals, like salespeople, so often have a reputation for operating from transaction-based and price-driven mindsets.

When customers talk about sellers, they often call them "vendors." The label "vendor" suggests a sell-side relationship. A machine can vend, and most salespeople are seen as vendors, too. The concept of supplier, however, extends beyond someone who just sells products and services. There is the added implication that suppliers provide customers with something they need and want. Supplying goods and services also suggests an ongoing relationship, a partnership that is based on more than a single transaction. Business customers see the best salespeople as suppliers.

Do you see your customers as buyers? Do you see yourself as a vendor or a supplier? And most important, how do your customers see you—as a vendor or as a supplier?

designation "world class" from business customers. But there is also a deeper reality at work here.

We know that customers see the products and services that salespeople offer them in terms of solutions. These solutions are intended to provide a specific set of outcomes. So, when customers buy solutions, they are actually buying the outcomes. Theodore Levitt, one of the great thinkers in the discipline of marketing, cited a simple example that speaks to this conclusion perfectly. People do not want to buy quarter-inch drill bits, he wrote. They want to buy quarter-inch holes.[24]

If customers are buying Levitt's quarter-inch drill bits, we can assume that they are planning to make the holes themselves. But what happens when you take the analogy out of the hardware store and into the world of business-to-business sales with products and services that are often highly complex? In this world, you are most often dealing with customers who are not sure whether holes are what they really need, or who may not know how to make holes even when they have the drill bit in hand, or who do not want to make them because they have far better uses for their time. The odds that these customers will get the outcomes they want by simply buying Levitt's drill bits don't look all that attractive.

These business customers need help. They are interested in acquiring value in some form or another, and they want to work with someone who will help ensure that they get it. In essence, they are looking for someone who can manage an element of their business that they have chosen to outsource, whether it is a simple part or an entire business process. This is, in fact, what your customers are doing wherever they buy anything from you. Instead of manufacturing a product internally (such as Nike's sneakers), or providing a service (such as plant security) themselves, they are outsourcing it to you.

Customers turn to you, the salesperson who is their primary and, sometimes, sole contact point, to oversee this outsourced element of their business. They are engaging you to manage a process of value acquisition as it relates to whatever it is that they purchased from you. Your customers want you to be accountable for this aspect of their business that you are supplying. They expect you to act as their *business agent.*

There are all kinds of business agents. Many of them, such as literary agents, talent agents, and financial planners, manage specific elements of an individual client's affairs. Others, such as CPAs, PR agents, and lawyers, manage elements of their corporate clients' businesses. Independent sales reps and insurance brokers are also business agents, at least in the sense that they represent the product lines of their client companies. They are managing portions of their client's sales and distribution processes.

One thing that these agents all have in common is that they accept the responsibility for managing some element of their clients' business, whether it is investments or media exposure or legal affairs. Another commonality is that they act as representatives of their clients. Even though they operate independently, they are presumed to act in and for their client's interest. The agents' self-interests are presumed to be aligned with and secondary to their clients' interests. When business agents act in ways that serve themselves well but not their clients, they are acting improperly, unethically, and in some cases, illegally.

Customers tell us that world-class salespeople act exactly like those agents who are fulfilling their obligations properly. Like business agents, these salespeople are not their employees, and usually, they have other customers. Like business agents, these salespeople are responsible for managing an outsourced piece of their business, whether it is office supplies or enterprise-level software systems, and for ensuring the customer's satisfaction. And, like business agents, these salespeople are trusted to act in accordance with their customers' interests.

This might sound like all expectation and no reward, but our studies reveal that when salespeople act as business agents, they win along with their customers. When they provide the service and outcomes that their customers expect, they are very well rewarded in terms of the share of the customer's wallet, long-term customer loyalty, and referrals to new prospective customers.

If you think of yourself as your customer's business agent, would it alter your approach to selling? Would you continue to sell the way you are selling today? What, if anything, would you do differently? The answers to these questions will depend on how you see your role in the creation and fulfillment of the sales contract that you help establish between your company and your customer.

Managing the Sale in the Role of Business Agent

In at least one sense, almost all salespeople are already acting as managers. Selling is a process in and of itself. Although the leaders of the sales organization usually determine how this process works, salespeople are responsible for executing it and leading potential customers through its steps. In this sense, salespeople are like line managers. They may not make the strategic-level decisions, but they manage a process that supports their company's strategic vision and plan.

While all sales processes require at least some managerial skill to execute properly, some are less well aligned than others to the salesperson's role as a business agent who represents the customer. Traditional sales processes, for instance, are heavily oriented toward a sell-side perspective. They are product-based. That is, they rely heavily on communicating the features and benefits of the product or service you are selling. These processes are not overly focused on customers, who are presumed to be quite capable of taking care of themselves.

Still, even these rather limited processes require that you manage yourself and your customers as you travel through the sales process together. Depending on the sales environment in which you are working, you might need to manage the prospect identification and qualification process; plan and make initial customer contact; prepare, schedule, and deliver sales presentations; and orchestrate the closing of the sale. By the way, traditional *qualify-present-close* sales processes can produce good results, so long as customers only need, and want, to know about the product's features and benefits in order to make sound decisions, are fully capable of looking out for their own interests, and can achieve the outcomes they desire on their own. For these reasons, they tend to be most commonly seen in simple commodity-type sales.

However, the business agent role that customers increasingly expect salespeople to assume *does not* play a large part in traditional sales processes. We believe that this is the primary reason why so many business-to-business sales organizations have abandoned such traditional processes. The shift first appeared in the more complex business-to-business markets. It is easy to see why. Compare, for instance, the considerations inherent in deciding whether or not to buy an innovative business intelligence software system that has just appeared on the market versus the considerations in buying nuts and bolts for an assembly operation. It is obvious that the former is a sale in which customers are highly likely to require expert assistance in making their decision to buy. It is also obvious that the salesperson is the logical source of this guidance. The problem is that if salespeople are using traditional sales processes and acting in the traditional sales role, they are *not* focused on providing that guidance.

Client-centered sales processes, such as Neil Rackham's SPIN Selling, Jeff Thull's Diagnostic Business Development, and Michael Bosworth's Solution Selling, have been developed to help provide customers with this elusive expertise and assistance.[25] These processes require that salespeople adopt the consultative role of a business agent to consummate a sale. They offer a mechanism and teach salespeople how to help their customers understand and quantify their problems, define their needs, explore solution alternatives, and reach the best purchase decisions. By the way, the customer's willingness to trust in and cooperate with the salesperson is critical to the success of these processes. Customers do not necessarily have to have a high level of trust in a salesperson when the salesperson is describing simple product features and benefits that are easily verified. When customers must provide salespeople with confidential information, however, as well as accept the results of analyses that they may not fully understand in addition to the risks inherent in so many complex and expensive solutions, the salesperson's integrity becomes a critical factor in the outcome of the sale. Likewise, you cannot be an effective business agent if your customers do not trust you.

So, in complex sales, in which the customer depends on the salesperson for the expertise needed to analyze and manage the purchase, client-centered approaches are a matter of necessity. Interestingly, though, so-called commodity sellers also are switching to client-centered selling approaches. In fact, these techniques are even popping up in retail sales. For example, big-box electronics retailer Best Buy is in the process of teaching its salespeople to differentiate its customers based on a series of consumer profiles. It has identified five segments of customers, such as the "affluent professional," the "family man," and the "busy suburban mom," and it is teaching its sales staff to recognize and sell to them based on their different needs and desires.[26]

Why are so many commodity sellers and even retailers adopting client-centered sales processes? It is a matter of added value and differentiation. Commodity salespeople are raising the level of their game by using client-centered selling and are acting more like business agents. As Bob Boyer from specialty paper manufacturer P. H. Glatfelter Company said in one of our studies, "The only difference between some products is the people who sell them."

Expanding into Post-Sale Activities

A salesperson knocks on the door of a prospective customer and offers to provide something of value. The prospect decides to buy that value. What does the salesperson do next? Your answer, according to what customers tell us, is a major determinant in how long they will remain your customers and how much of their business they will award to you.

It turns out that when customers say that world-class salespeople are personally accountable for results, most often they are talking about the management of *post-sale* activities. There may be some customer satisfaction involved in making a decision to buy, but to most customers, it is more like a leap of faith. When they sign the sales contract, they are expressing faith in the ability of the salesperson and his or her company to provide a solution to an existing problem or some new opportunity. It is the first step in a fulfillment process that they *hope* will result in substantiated value. True satisfaction, the kind that translates into loyalty and repeat business, comes later, if and when they have actually received the value they had hoped to acquire.

Most business-to-business salespeople, on the other hand, tend not to think in those terms. We find that salespeople fall into three categories when it comes to post-sale activities:

- **Closers:** Most salespeople belong to this first category. In it, salespeople take responsibility for the sales process up to the signing of the contract. They may also deliver the purchased goods themselves or confirm that the purchase is delivered.
- **Maintainers:** Fewer salespeople, but still a substantial number, fall into this second category. They add installation and use to their job descriptions and provide product service and support. They make sure the customer's purchase is installed and continues to work. If it requires periodic service and/or consumes something that must be replaced, they ensure that it is properly maintained.

- **Outcome managers:** Almost invariably, world-class salespeople belong to this third, least populated, category. In it, salespeople take responsibility for the ultimate end benefit that the customer hopes to receive. In other words, the salespeople's goals are aligned with their customers' results.

Whether they are selling office supplies or the administration of a 401(k) plan or the implementation of a CRM package that enables the customer's service reps to cross-sell and upsell its own customers, the best salespeople are always striving to manage the sale at this third and highest level of accountability. This kind of salesperson works hard to ensure that the value purchased is realized—that the right office supplies are in the storage cabinets in the right quantities at the right price; that the customer's employees receive the information they need to adjust the mix of their investments when financial conditions change; that the customer's call center is actually generating the new sales and the higher levels of customer satisfaction that the CRM software was supposed to facilitate.

Why aren't more salespeople working at this highest level of accountability? Perhaps it is because they and their companies do not recognize the rewards that await them there. Business-to-business sellers tend to be overly, and unhealthily, focused on new business. They often view a sale to new customers as somehow more valuable than a sale to an existing customer. Sometimes, they actually reward "closer" behavior, paying higher commissions on new business than on repeat business. The champagne corks pop when they close a new piece of business, but in fact, they should be celebrating the business they receive from existing customers instead.

New business is still important—every company needs to build its customer base—but because of the additional cost involved in winning new business, repeat business is almost always more profitable. A 2004 McKinsey report, for instance, calculated that on average it costs ten times *less* to do business with an existing customer than it does to acquire a new one.[27] The revenues associated with repeat customers also rise in greater increments. Studies reported in *Harvard Business Review* concluded that a 5 percent rise in customer retention rates increased sales by a minimum of 25 percent.[28] In some industries, it is far higher, such as software (35 percent), industrial distribution (45 percent), credit cards (75 percent), and advertising (95 percent).

In addition to not valuing repeat business properly, sellers also tend to underestimate the impact that customer satisfaction levels have on repeat business. Eighty percent of all companies *deserting* their previous vendors described their satisfaction levels as ranging from "good" to "very good" in another study reported in *Harvard Business Review*.[29] Conversely, those with satisfaction levels starting at "very good" and ranging up to "excellent" were 42 percent more likely to continue the relationship. In other words, the fact that you have made a sale in no way guarantees that you will be able to keep the customer.

All of these findings support the fact that, if you aren't already, you should be considering how to manage post-sales activities and ensure that your customers attain their desired outcomes. This requires a wider view of the relationship with customers, one that encompasses the full breadth of a customer's interactions with your company. It is worth it. The panoramic view that includes the full extent of your company's contract with the customer includes the richest potential for profit, a potential that resides outside the traditional sales paradigm.

Three Competencies for Results Accountability

All of the skills we describe in this book support the work of personally managing your customers' results, but three of those skills stand out in business customers' minds. They tell us that the best salespeople serve as a single point of contact, provide the

---

THE PEAK/END RULE

The way in which our brains process experiences also supports the need for a strong post-sales effort. Nobel Prize–winning psychologist Daniel Kahneman found that humans tend to evaluate their experiences based on their emotional peaks and their endings, no matter what else happens in between. He conducted experiments that revealed that positive endings lessen our perceptions of any prior unpleasantness. He calls it the *Peak/End Rule*, and it's one more reason why paying attention to the sale's end game can pay great dividends.

---

full range of expertise needed to ensure value, and are accountable for value and ROI. These three skills carry the greatest weight in the fulfillment of the first customer rule.

Skill #1: Making Yourself the Single Point of Contact

In 1952, Frank Perdue became president of Perdue Farms, a $6 million egg farm on Maryland's Eastern Shore founded by his father three decades before. He expanded the business into fresh poultry and grain products, and then, in 1968, opened the company's first integrated processing plant. When Perdue passed away on March 31, 2005, the still privately owned business had grown into the third-largest poultry company in the United States, with more than 20,000 employees and revenues of $2.8 billion in 2004.

What drove this growth? Certainly, Perdue went to extraordinary lengths to provide the perfect bird. He discovered that customers wanted chickens with yellow skin, hairless wings, and meatier breasts, and he made sure they got them. But as Joseph Nocera wrote in the *New York Times*, "Still, a Perdue chicken is, in the end, just a chicken."[30] So what was it that made Perdue so successful? The short answer is advertising. Over twenty-four years, he appeared in roughly 200 commercials, becoming a celebrity in the process. "It takes a tough man to make a tender chicken," Perdue told us. He explained why his chickens were the best in the universe and that he stood behind them. In effect, Perdue provided his customers with the first single point of contact they had ever had when buying chicken, and they responded. Nocera concluded, "He thought he was selling chickens. But he was selling Frank Perdue."

Like Frank Perdue, business agents provide a single point of contact. If you use a financial advisor to manage your personal

CONTACT MEANS COMMUNICATION

Being a single point of contact requires that you be a highly effective communicator. Here is a set of profile points that identify effective communicators, as derived from the HR Chally Group's assessment database of more than 300,000 salespeople. How do you measure up?

1. Is sensitive to the customer's circumstances and response, adjusting the communication of information or ideas to accommodate the customer's need to know and/or level of understanding.
2. Encourages questions, comments, and feedback from the customer.
3. Gives specific details of how, who, and when, promising that the complexity of delivery and servicing of the product line will be shouldered by the salesperson.
4. Keeps the focus on content and substance, not flash and performance.
5. Talks with the customer, creating a team feeling of working together, versus directing a speech at the customer.

assets, you expect that person to be your point of contact. The advisor may recommend that you invest your savings in a variety of assets, but if you have any issues with those investments, you call the advisor, not the various providers. Business customers tell us that they expect the same single point of contact in their vendor relationships. They expect the salesperson to be the first person they are going to need to talk to, and often the only one. They do not want to be forced to negotiate their way through a series of contacts, departments, and transfers to achieve satisfaction.

The importance of seeing the bigger picture and thinking beyond product features and benefits supports your ability to serve as an effective customer contact point. You cannot be a knowledgeable contact point unless and until you are able to:

- Understand the customer's goals
- Make recommendations in accordance with those goals
- Manage the process through which the goals are reached
- Provide warnings when those goals are threatened for any reason

As we have seen, in your customers' minds you are an external source of value that they are hiring to accomplish a task that they either cannot or do not wish to manage themselves. They see your company as an outsourced department of their companies and they see you as the manager of that department. In viewing you as an outsourced manager or a business agent, your customers' expectations begin with your acting as their single point of contact, but they do not end there. Your customers also expect you to provide expertise, which is the second skill in personally managing customer results.

Skill #2: Managing Teams of Experts

In many business-to-business sales, it is unrealistic to expect that the salespeople themselves will or can have all of the expertise that customers might require. These are sales that often involve financial, legal, design, and/or technological assessments that are well beyond any one person's capabilities. Happily, customers do not expect salespeople to be expert in each of these areas themselves. They do, however, expect salespeople to identify and recruit experts as needed and manage them as they provide their expertise to the customer.

Accordingly, when we benchmark world-class salespeople, we find that they often do not deliver results personally. Instead, they oversee, facilitate, and confirm the delivery of expertise. They act as outsourced managers who are responsible for other outsourced employees. Schwab Institutional Senior Vice President Nick Georgis alluded to this when he told us: "The new and most critical role of the salesperson will be to manage the relationship with the customer and not to execute the various action steps."

The reality is that business-to-business selling is becoming a team effort, and the best salespeople are acting as team leaders. Usually, these sales teams are not permanent. Their membership shifts as the customer's need for expertise evolves and fluctuates. They are virtual sales teams in which members come together as needed and disband when their work is done. As managers of the entire business relationship, salespeople do not focus on becoming the experts as much as they invest their resources in knowing how to access and manage the expertise of others. The best salespeople are prepared to call upon expert resources wherever they may be located within their companies to help plan, execute, and troubleshoot the solutions they are selling to their customers.

This emerging approach to selling does require that salespeople assume the authority needed to manage a team of experts. This can be a difficult task in and of itself, as Hewlett-Packard recently discovered. In late 2003, in the quest to reduce the number of calls that salespeople from different H-P businesses were making on the same business customers and to ensure that the customers were offered a complete bundle of H-P's products and services, Carly Fiorina created the Customer Solutions Group (CSG). CSG was a standalone sales group that answered directly to the CEO's office and was responsible for all of the company's enterprise, small, and medium-sized business, and public sector customers worldwide. The group never produced the bump in sales that was expected. Two years later, when Fiorina was forced out of H-P and replaced by Mark Hurd, a former salesperson himself, the new CEO quickly made the decision to dissolve CSG and merge the sales function back into the company's three major business units: Imaging and Printing, Personal Systems, and Technology Solutions. Why?

It appears that the problem was that no one had authority over the entire sales team and as a result, sales could not be completed because of constraints within H-P itself. "Part of it is the fact that multiple people show up lacking accountability and lacking responsibility at the point of contact," explained Hurd during a 2005 interview, "And I really don't think it's the people's fault. I think it's the fact that the model doesn't allow enough ownership at the point of contact and enough clarity of responsibility and simplification of the model."[31] Hurd said that he embedded H-P's sales forces back into the product groups "not just so we can improve our cost structure, but so we can make decisions, get a price to the customer, get a quote to the customer, a line of resource to a customer—so we can get on with getting on."

The idea that the authority of salespeople has a positive impact on revenue generation is supported by a number of academic studies. One of them focused on the acceptance of new products among professional buyers at retail food stores in the United States, Japan, and South Korea. It was discovered that, in the highly competitive struggle to get shelf space for new products, "the power of the salesperson has a strong impact on the retail buyer's trust in the salesperson in all three countries."[32] It turns out that customers see a salesperson's power as the ability to get things done, which translates to greater trust that the salesperson will get things done, which in turn translates into higher sales of new products. Among the study's recommendations: empower salespeople in terms of authority and decision-making.

The best salespeople demonstrate their ability to lead the sales team by:

- Serving as the central point for decision-making on customer issues
- Mobilizing and coordinating supplier teams to provide expertise and resources for the sale
- Ensuring that each team member understands the proposed solution and how it will be used in the customer's business

So, thus far, you know that you must be a single point of contact and manage the expertise required in the sale, but toward what end? What is it that actually determines the customer's satisfaction? It is value and ROI, and that is where the third skill for personally managing the customer's results comes in.

Skill #3: Being the ROI Expert

The traditional vision of sales has been driven by the concept of volume. More sales volume equals more revenue, and more revenue equals more profit. It sounds right on the surface, but it is dangerously simplistic. In fact, there are times when higher sales volume can be a fast track to disaster. If you are selling a product or service whose margins are not high enough to generate a profit or that dissatisfies your customers, increasing your sales volume can quickly create a self-perpetuating negative performance spiral. What is missing here is customer value. That is what should be driving your sales efforts, not volume.

Customers, of course, do not care about your sales volume. As we've seen, however, one of their three fundamental wants is "substantiated value." If you deliver enough customer value to entice customers to pay more, you can maintain and increase sales margins. In that case, customer value begets sales success and corporate profitability. It also drives sales volume because when customers achieve value from their purchases, they return to buy again and they spread the word to other potential customers. As Don Peppers and Martha Rogers, who first introduced the idea of 1to1 marketing, say, "You can only create lasting value for your company by first creating lasting value for customers."[33]

If customer satisfaction and loyalty are driven by value, it is clear that one of the most important skills you can develop is the ability to communicate, deliver, and measure the value your products and services bring to customers. You must become an ROI expert and embrace responsibility for ensuring that your customers achieve the returns they have been promised. Think of it as taking accountability for the profit-and-loss statement of whichever department you have been hired to manage as the customer's business agent.

Metrics is a key word in describing this skill. Too often, when we talk about managing customer relationships, satisfaction,

---

SATISFACTION AND LOYALTY

Customer satisfaction is transactional in nature. Every interaction a customer has with your company can produce satisfaction or dissatisfaction. But a single satisfactory experience is not enough to produce customer loyalty. Loyalty results from the accumulation of satisfactory experiences; in other words, the continual and consistent experience of satisfaction evolves into customer loyalty. World-class salespeople understand the relationship between customer satisfaction and customer loyalty. They deliver transactional satisfaction in the quest for long-term loyalty.

and loyalty, it sounds "soft." But world-class salespeople understand that business relationships and customer satisfaction and loyalty are not built on good feelings. Rather, good feelings are one result of relationships that are built on quantifiable value and expressed in metrics that accurately reflect the customer's needs and desires. For instance, when we benchmarked Applied Industrial Technologies, one of the world-class sales forces identified in our studies, we found that its sales force had created a Documented Value-Added program, which vice president Rick Shaw described as "a process we use to document for customers the value we add in terms of generating uptime, eliminating downtime and providing emergency service, cost savings and much more."

The best salespeople demonstrate their value and ROI expertise by:

- Considering the economics of their customers' processes
- Proactively weighing decisions, recommendations, and actions against their impact on the customer's bottom line
- Offering customers options that accomplish their goals without compromising profitability
- Accurately measuring and reporting the value their customers achieve

Not only does the recognition of value and ROI enable salespeople to sell more effectively, it also enables them to more effectively manage post-sale activities. They can set schedules and ensure that they are on track for meeting deadlines. If they are measuring the value received by the customer, they know when the solution is not working as planned and can proactively respond to problems. Value expertise creates the foundation for prompt and efficient response.

Salespeople who become value and ROI experts are also able to more effectively penetrate customer accounts. As Doug Duncan of Roadway explained it to us: "Once you find a customer, you have to figure out a way to put locks around him or her by adding continuous value to that relationship. The more customers you keep, the more selective you can be with new ones. This is a yield strategy as well as a revenue strategy." When you recognize the value you offer customers and can quantify its achievement, you can build long-term sales plans for the customers and time your new offers to coincide with their needs. Further, customers tell us that when they have received the value they expected from previously purchased solutions, they have every reason to consider these offers in a favorable light.

Interestingly, the very act of becoming a value and ROI expert increases the value you yourself can bring to your customers. You become more than a conduit of value. In providing this information, you become a source of value, too.

The ability to provide your customers with value and ROI expertise in the quest to be personally accountable for their results leads us directly to the second customer rule. You cannot recognize customer value until you understand the customer's business. Here's how Xerox CEO Anne Mulcahy, who started as a field sales representative with the company in 1976 and has been credited with saving the company from bankruptcy in the tough post-millennial economy, put it: "Really having a great customer relationship means that you understand the customer's business well enough to solve something that is important to them, that helps their bottom line or their top line."[34] That is the topic of our next chapter.

CHAPTER 4

"You Must Understand Our Business"

On June 27, 2003, the Federal Trade Commission launched the National Do Not Call Registry, a database intended to help eliminate unwanted residential telephone sales calls. In four days, irritated and frustrated Americans registered more than 10 million telephone numbers. Within forty days, more than 30 million numbers were registered. On August 18, 2005, the 100 millionth telephone number was registered.[35] It was a clear and unequivocal message about the desirability of the sales calls Americans were receiving at home.

Based on what business customers have been telling us about the sales calls they receive, it is a good thing that there is not a Do Not Call Registry in which they can register their work numbers. Business customers are receiving more sales calls than ever and, since the FTC has not yet offered them relief, the customers have responded by making it more difficult for business-to-business sellers to establish direct contact. They are using their receptionists, assistants, and voice-mail systems to protect themselves from unwanted calls. But if business-to-business sellers are providing solutions that are capable of creating value, why are their prospective customers hunkering down behind such barricades?

The answer is that too many of the sales calls that customers receive are not relevant to their situations and their needs. At the Chally Group, we constantly get sales calls like these. Our business depends on computers and computing power, but because our needs are specialized and our staff has the required expertise, we build our own equipment. We buy computer parts, not computers. Yet, we receive a stream of calls from PC and server salespeople who want to sell us their machines. Naturally, we have a soft spot for salespeople, and as a result, we are more tolerant of inappropriate sales calls than is the typical business customer. However, we are not going to buy products and services we cannot use just because we empathize with salespeople and the challenging nature of their work. (Even if we *did* buy computers, we would be reluctant to work with salespeople who are clearly more interested in talking about their products than in understanding our computing needs.)

The lesson to keep in mind here: For business customers, the most important question is never whether or not your products and services are capable of delivering value. It is whether or not your customers need and can use the value being offered.

If you talk with the executives in your company, you will surely find that they get a tremendous number of irrelevant sales calls, too. When you talk to them, listen for this complaint about the salespeople who make the calls: "They don't understand our business." You might hear this sentiment in any number of different forms, but no matter what the exact phrasing, it is among the most frequent of all the complaints that we hear from business customers.

This problem was revealed in our studies anecdotally. When we begin creating our surveys, we ask customers open-ended questions, such as, "What was the reason you left your previous vendor, and was there anything about the salesperson that contributed to that?" When we asked that specific question, the most common response was that the salesperson's failure to understand the customer's business had undermined the relationship.

These comments were not just the peevish outbursts of managers and executives who had been interrupted during the course of a busy workday by an inappropriate cold call. The salesperson's inability and/or unwillingness to understand the customer's business creates a fundamental barrier to effective selling. The ability to understand a customer's company structure, operations, competitive environment, and financial results and concerns supports everything you do as a business-to-business salesperson. You cannot manage customer satisfaction, provide applications, solve problems, and create innovative solutions if you do not understand the customer's world. Understanding the customer's business is the foundation for customer-centric selling. As Dan Garrett, vice president and managing partner at Computer Sciences Corporation's Global Health Solutions, says, "To avoid being transactionally based, you must take the time to understand both your client's business and the industry in which it operates. This involves taking a close look under the

---

GMAC UNDERSTANDS THE CUSTOMER'S BUSINESS

The salespeople in GMAC's auto financing division call on the F&I (finance and insurance) managers at car dealerships throughout the nation. F&I managers are salespeople themselves. They sell the products and services—the loans, leases, insurance, extended warranties, and so on—that customers are offered after they decide to buy a new or used car. As with great salespeople everywhere, the best F&I managers are in high demand and often are courted and won away by other dealerships. GMAC's salespeople are so well trained in their customer's businesses that they will actually take over the F&I manager's daily responsibilities while a dealership searches for a new manager.

---

covers to figure out not just how to serve your client and your client's client, but also the industry as a whole."

When we ask business customers to describe world-class salespeople, they talk about the ability of these salespeople to communicate in the vernacular of the customer's company and industry, to speak knowledgeably to the issues and needs of the customer (sometimes, before the customer has fully realized those issues and needs), and to integrate themselves into the customer's company. The fundamental skill behind all of these capabilities is also the driving force behind the second customer rule: *"You must understand our business."*

Seeing Customers from a CEO Perspective

Like the other customer rules, the second rule has arisen in response to the changing nature of business-to-business sales. Advances in technology now allow processes that salespeople once executed, such as the provision of product information and order entry and tracking, to be completed over the Internet or remotely by other personnel. These advances have liberated salespeople from many rote administrative tasks. But at the same time, employers are placing increasing pressure on salespeople to spend this freed-up time getting closer to the customer and focusing on solutions and their benefits. Customers, as we have seen, also want salespeople to refocus their efforts. They want salespeople to act more like managers and understand all of the ramifications of the sale; lead the additional technical, logistics, and project management specialists who support the sale; and take accountability for results.

These new demands have forced salespeople to elevate their point of contact within the customers' businesses and to work with executives at higher levels. They have also placed increasing emphasis on the business case—the value and ROI that their solutions provide. All of this requires a more sophisticated understanding of their customers' businesses. As Gar Smith, general sales manager at GM Parts, told *Selling Power* magazine after his organization was identified in our 1998 survey, "Dealers expect GM people to come into their place of business and add value. To do that, you have to know what makes the dealership tick."[36]

More evidence of the need to know what makes your customers' businesses "tick" was revealed when we compared the results of our first survey, begun in 1992, with our Year 2000 study. Customers reported that the frequency with which CEOs and senior executives of business-to-business sellers were taking an active role in sales had risen exponentially. In 1992, senior executives were participating in only 8 percent of sales. By 2000, senior executives were participating in 22 percent of sales.

The authority of senior executives is one reason why we are seeing an increase in their participation in sales activities. We know that customers want to work with people who can not only make relevant sales promises, but who have the power to keep them, too. Certainly, senior leaders of the seller's organization qualify in that regard. But executives also bring an important skill to the table, a skill that is increasingly important and, too often, in short supply among salespeople.

What is this skill that your CEO has and you do not? Generally speaking, CEOs and other executives understand businesses and their issues better than salespeople. Their job includes profit-and-loss responsibility. They grapple with the implications of organizational structure and corporate culture on performance. They are charged with creating and executing strategy.

Most CEOs and other executives have been formally educated and trained to understand and run businesses. In addition, their daily responsibilities have given them a valuable experience base that they can draw upon to help the customer. They have the perspective, knowledge, and background needed to connect with a customer's business. When they meet with a prospective or existing customer, they can see those issues as the customer sees them.

ARROGANCE IS THE ENEMY OF UNDERSTANDING

We all have met people who are too smart for their good. They are enamored with their expertise, which they exhibit whenever the opportunity arises, even if they have to manufacture that opportunity themselves. And how do other people react to this behavior? Often, they interpret it as a superiority complex and they see the expert as arrogant. They withdraw from the self-styled expert.

Salespeople need to understand their customers' companies with a CEO's business savvy, but at the same time, they need to avoid behaviors that smack of arrogance. Their knowledge is meant to enhance their relationships with customers and to open the way for deeper and more meaningful interaction. Salespeople also need to recognize that no matter how much they know, their customers always know more about their own businesses.

Avoid the arrogance trap by never believing you have all the answers, and by not being afraid to say "I don't know . . ." when you don't. Be open to learning something new, and make your interest in your customers' businesses as clear as you can. Don't presume to know what the customers are experiencing until they tell you so.

They can ask the right questions and contribute insights and advice that address those issues. In short, they are business savvy.

On the other hand, business customers tell us that most salespeople are not particularly business savvy. We have already seen that their educational needs have been largely unaddressed by colleges and universities. Further, the employer-provided training that salespeople receive is mostly directed to product-focused sales skills, goal management, and motivation. This is not to say, however, that you cannot become business savvy. In fact, business customers tell us that the best salespeople already are.

Usually, these salespeople have not had the benefit of a formal education and training in business management. Typically, they have developed their understanding of their customer's businesses from time on the job and from the colleagues and sales managers who advised and mentored them. Like the CEO, the best salespeople have attained and developed the skills they need to recognize and speak to the customer's business issues. They are able to size up the company, identify and understand its business issues, and speak in terms of the results toward which the customer is driving. That is why we say that the best salespeople have adopted the role of the CEO.

There is one caveat here: Business issues undergo subtle changes according to the customer's position in the business. Plant managers and their CEOs deal with the same issues, but in a different light and with different emphasis. When we say that world-class salespeople understand a business as a CEO would, we do not mean to say that they talk to a plant manager as a CEO would. An effective salesperson speaks directly to a plant manager's concerns in that manager's terms, but the highest level of business understanding informs what the salesperson says.

Of course, there are practical limits to the knowledge that you can obtain, absorb, and use. Even CEOs, contrary to the posturing of those leaders whose egos may get the better of them, do not know everything there is to know about business. So, let's explore two parameters—one based on a generic understanding of the customer and one based on a customized understanding of the customer—that can help define the type and depth of customer knowledge you will need to achieve sales success.

How Your Markets Define Your Knowledge Needs

The first parameter of customer understanding is market-based. This knowledge is determined by the market segments you call upon and the kinds of customers that compose those segments. A market segmentation strategy, which is based on what your company sells to whom, divides up customers based on some set of attributes, such as location, size, industry, or technological needs, among others. In turn, this segmentation usually dictates how the sales force is organized, and which customers you are assigned to call upon, as well as the kinds of customer knowledge you need. Among the sales forces we have studied, this tends to break down into three broad categories, each of which is based on selling to a different type of market.

Category #1: Vertical Knowledge

If you sell goods and services to one industry or industry sector, you need to develop a vertical knowledge of the companies within that industry. Sellers of specialty papers are a good example. One of their largest markets is printers. No two printers are exactly identical. Some specialize in retail printing, such as invitations; others in commercial jobs, such as catalogs. Some provide a wide range of product and services; others specialize in one or two, such as business cards and letterhead. Nevertheless, all printers are very similar to one another.

When all of your customers are in essentially the same business, your market knowledge can be relatively narrow and very deep. Think of it as a vertical cut. You only need to understand one kind of business, but you want to become an expert on what it takes to be successful in that business. You can home in on the common set of problems, issues, and economic challenges that all of these customers face.

Category #2: Horizontal Knowledge

If you sell goods and services that cross industry boundaries, you need to develop horizontal market knowledge. Sellers of payroll services are a good example here. One of their largest markets is composed of major, employee-intensive corporations. But these businesses may have very little in common, except for the fact that they all must pay their employees.

If you are selling payroll services to enterprise-level customers, your market knowledge can be wide, but relatively shallow. Think of it as a horizontal cut across your customers' businesses. You would want to become an expert on the payroll process as it relates to all large companies. You can learn everything about payroll accounting and the associated issues of concern to your customers' finance departments.

Because your customers' businesses will vary so widely, horizontal knowledge usually creates additional complexity. So, you may need to understand how payroll practices vary among industries and how they differ in union and non-union environments. Since the laws and regulations regarding payroll vary by state, you may also need knowledge that is geographically specific.

Category #3: Specialized Knowledge

Finally, if you sell goods and services that address niche markets, you need to develop highly specialized knowledge. Sellers of medical devices are a good example here. Your sole market might be neurosurgeons, or even just neurosurgeons who specialize in one specific set of procedures. Generally speaking, these are customers who are virtually identical and who will use your solution in the same ways.

If you are selling a specialized product to a niche market, your market knowledge can be precisely targeted and very deep. You will want to become an expert in the customer's use of your solution. If you sell medical devices that are surgically implanted, for instance, you might learn how to do the operation. In fact, these types of salespeople are often charged with "in-servicing" responsibilities. They are present in operating theaters and they train and advise surgeons in the use of their products, particularly when new devices are introduced and used for the first time. Often, the salespeople actually participate. Sales representatives for pacemaker manufacturers calibrate and test their devices as part of the implantation procedure.[37]

So, the first parameter of customer understanding is concerned with the larger view of the markets in which your customers operate and the knowledge that requires. This can include understanding issues such as market shifts, the competitive threats that your customer faces, and/or the regulatory environment. It also includes understanding the business and process models commonly used in your customers' industries. Finally, it can mean an in-depth understanding of exactly how your customer segment is using your products and services.

MARKET KNOWLEDGE BUILDS SALES CREDIBILITY

Often, salespeople fail to recognize the insights into their markets that their positions afford them. As you travel between customers, trade shows, and association meetings within the customer's industries and/or functional specialties, you are exposed to trends and issues with which your individual customers may not yet be familiar. Answering these questions can help you build the market knowledge that can build your credibility with customers:

- Currently, what are the issues of most concern in your customers' industries?
- What are the emerging challenges within those industries?
- What problems are creating the greatest degree of confusion among your customers?
- How are the industry leaders addressing these issues, challenges, and problems?
- What solutions are your competitors, industry experts, and academicians proposing?
- How do your products and services relate to the issues, challenges, and problems?
- How do your products and services relate to the solutions?

The Three Facets of Corporate Knowledge

The second parameter of customer understanding relates to business customers as individual companies. Because it delves into attributes that are unique to an individual customer as opposed to a segment of customers, this knowledge applies no matter what and/or where your markets are. These are the attributes that set one customer apart from your other customers. This parameter defines the knowledge needed to analyze the customer's company, to create an internal portrait of that business, and to create and deliver customized solutions.

For the purposes of sales, we can break down the kinds of knowledge needed to understand an individual customer's business into three components:

1. *Understanding the customer's customers and/or the beneficiaries of your solutions.* This is knowledge that you require to understand how you can help your customers succeed by better serving their customers.

2. *Understanding the "health" of the customer's company.* This is knowledge that you require to act as a surrogate manager and align yourself effectively with the customer's organizational strategy, structure, and culture.

3. *Understanding the customer's financial condition.* This is knowledge that you require to understand the viability of the prospect as a customer, to identify the degree of impact your solutions can offer, to connect solutions to substantiated value, and to quantify solution results.

Let's explore each of these facets of corporate understanding in greater detail and see how you can put them to work in your quest to better understand and serve your customers.

Your Customer's Customers and Other Value Beneficiaries

The business world is a long value chain. Your company buys products and services and uses them to create value. You sell that value in your company's products and services. When you are successful, your customers buy your products and services, use them to create new products and services, and sell them to their customers. Their customers may be the end users, or the value chain may continue for another link or more. The salient point here is that your customers have customers just as you do, and those customers are, or should be, the focus of everything they do, as your customers are for you.

As the business world becomes more and more customer-centric, one of the most compelling skills you can bring to the sale is the ability to help your customers better serve their customers. There is no greater motivator among business customers than the ability to grow their companies. When you can align the solutions you sell to the customer's customer, and help your customers better serve their own customers, you transcend sales and become a business partner. However, you cannot provide this level of service until you know who your customer's customers are, what they want, and how your products and services can help fulfill those wants.

BUILDING THE FOUNDATION OF CUSTOMER KNOWLEDGE

1. Research the customer's business.
2. Identify the company's key personnel and their backgrounds.
3. Learn the customer's organizational procedures and cultural preferences.
4. Document the important details so you are not dependent on memory.

Question #1: Who Are Your Customer's Customers?

Like your company, your customers are searching out ways to differentiate themselves from their competitors. To accomplish this goal, they may be using unique technologies that appeal to certain segments of their customer markets more than others. They also may have adopted business models that are designed to appeal to certain customers more than others. To begin to examine the first facet of corporate knowledge, you need to identify and define this unique set of customers that your customer is pursuing.

Think of how Dell Computer's approach to consumer PC sales differs from Hewlett-Packard's approach. Generally speaking, Dell is focused on direct marketing, while H-P is focused on sales through retailers. Like Dell, H-P's customers include the consumers who purchase their PCs. But unlike Dell, there is another set of customers to consider: the wholesale customers who buy, stock, and sell H-P's PCs in their stores. Both companies make and sell PCs, but their customer sets are different.

Next, you need to understand how your customer's unique set of customers is changing. Markets are always in flux, so you must ask yourself how changes in the markets your customers sell into are affecting their customer bases. What existing customer set is your customer struggling to retain? What new customer sets does it want to serve in the future?

To answer these questions, read your customers' marketing and sales literature. Who are they written for? Visit your customers' Web sites and read their descriptions of their customer markets and the customer success stories they post. With whom are they doing business?

Question #2: What Do Your Customer's Customers Want?

If you know what your customer's customers want, by definition you know what your customer wants. So, once you have identified your customers' customers, ask yourself what it is they are hoping to accomplish when they buy your customers' products and services. Ask yourself how they buy those products and services, and how other companies in your customers' industries are satisfying their customers' needs, wants, and demands. The answers to questions like these will provide you with insights into the customer challenges that your own customers are facing.

The ability to speak knowledgeably to the needs of your customers' customers is an instant credibility builder. It is also a wonderful source of ideas for innovation and improvement. Witness how often new products and services are developed by suppliers. Shippers, not grocers, created the self-replenishing, rear-loading refrigerators that facilitate the sale of perishable products like milk. Likewise, the misting systems that make the vegetables look so fresh and delicious came from shippers, not grocers. (Oddly, shippers did not invent the trailers that automatically unload pallets via a built-in conveyer system, which save time, wear and tear, and also allow for lighter construction. A grocer did.)

Question #3: How Does What You Sell Benefit Your Customer's Customers?

Sometimes, it is very clear how your products and services can support your customer's efforts to win new business and build the loyalty of its customer base. If you sell parts and subassemblies that go into finished goods or provide services that are bundled and resold, there is a direct line between you and your customer's customers. If you can offer improved performance or lowered cost, your customer can in turn offer its customers improved performance or lowered cost. In these cases, your primary emphasis would be to understand how your customer's customers use and value the contributions that you make to the products and services that your customer sells to them.

In other cases, the connection between your solutions and your customer's customers is less distinct. If you sell preventive maintenance software, you are offering your customer productivity improvements, such as gains in uptime. How do these benefits connect to your customer's customers? Well, they improve the quality of your customer's products and thus, the satisfaction and value that its customers receive. They also could translate into lower costs for your customer, and thus could enable lower prices for its own customers. Alternatively, the productivity gains might simply drop to your customer's bottom line and provide additional resources that it can devote to serving customers better. In these cases, your primary emphasis may be to understand the gain the customer will realize in operating efficiencies. Don't forget, however, that the connection to the customer's customers remains a strong consideration in the sale.

Finally, you might sell products or services that do not appear to address your customer's customers at all. If you sell landscaping services or print annual reports, for instance, the connection to the customer's customers might appear tenuous at best. But, in fact, there are also customer's customers here; they are stakeholders in your customer's business. Attractive landscaping can enhance a company's standing as a good neighbor within the community and make it more attractive to existing and potential employees. An annual report that dramatically communicates the customer's story can help it attract and retain investors. Often, these benefits will eventually translate into customer benefits. Employees who enjoy their workplace are likely to serve their customers better, for instance. In these cases, however, the more effective focus of your understanding would be the stakeholders. They are your customer's customers in the sense that they are beneficiaries of the value you are selling.

Strategy, Structure, and Culture

The second facet of corporate knowledge is the "health" of the customer's company. The health of a company (aside from its financial position, which we will explore as the third and final facet) is a portrait of its internal condition. This portrait includes the company's goals and how it is planning to attain them, the way it is organized, and the way people work together within it. In other words, it is the strategy, structure, and culture of your customer's company.

World-class salespeople are intensely interested in customer strategy, structure, and culture for very good reason. Each of these elements produces impacts that can support or undermine sales results. Further, these factors often play a large role in determining the long-term success of the customer's business, and that success often translates directly into the success of its suppliers and business partners. For example, in 1981, after IBM decided it would enter the PC market, it hired a small software company with annual revenues of less than $20 million, a company named Microsoft, to provide the operating system. By 1990, the IBM-compatible PC had become the industry standard and Microsoft's revenues had exceeded $1 billion annually.[38]

Strategy

A company's strategy tells the best salespeople about the company's viability as a potential customer in both the short and long term. The average salesperson sees a customer problem that his or her solutions could address, and proceeds with the sale. World-class salespeople, on the other hand, seek to identify where the customer's attention and resources are currently focused. They know that customers who are pursuing a well-defined strategy or struggling with large and compelling problems are unlikely prospects for any solution that does not directly address their concerns. Anyone selling high-tech products in 2000 and 2001 can tell you that customers who are faced with shrinking demand for their products and are desperately focused on reducing unused and unneeded capacity are not good prospects for state-of-the-art equipment that increases production rates and requires a large capital outlay.

Structure

The best salespeople also seek to understand the customer's corporate structure. The way in which a company is organized determines where and how quickly decisions are made. Highly bureaucratic companies may have abnormally long sales cycles, and the salesperson will plan and pace the sale accordingly. Flat structures, where there may be only two or three levels of management between the CEO and frontline employees, might require that salespeople move quickly to capture the opportunity. Companies that feature remote and hierarchical decision-making authority require a different sales strategy than those with local, decentralized command structures.

You can see the importance of understanding structure in one of the most common and unpleasant surprises in sales. How often have you seen salespeople walk away from a presentation with local executives fully expecting the sale is won, only to find out later that a senior decision-maker somewhere up the chain of command, whom they neither considered nor addressed, nixed it?

Culture

The culture of a company, like the culture of a nation, is composed of the values, norms, and beliefs shared by its leaders and employees. A company's culture determines "the way we do things here," and many studies have shown that cultural elements have a significant impact on corporate performance.[39] The best salespeople are highly attuned to corporate culture because it too affects a prospective customer's sales potential and the outcome of the sale. Think about the much-publicized contrast between the purchasing practices at General Motors and at Toyota in the late 1990s. Both companies were intensely focused on driving down costs, but their cultures were distinctly different. General Motors' purchasing staff became notorious for simply mandating fixed price reductions across the board and leaving suppliers to figure out how to absorb the loss. Toyota was committed to a cooperative, partnership approach and worked with its major suppliers to help them increase their manufacturing productivity and efficiency. A salesperson for an automotive supplier might call on both companies, but the sales approach would have to be very different at each company.

Making a Quick Diagnosis

When we benchmarked the sales forces that business customers identified as world-class, we discovered that the best salespeople are able to quickly identify the health factors of the companies they call upon. Sales executives in Boise Cascade's office supplies group, for instance, told us that their best salespeople could size up any large office on the first walkthrough. They could tell from visual and aural clues, such as the layout of the office and its cleanliness and neatness, whether it was a productive office or not. They could tell from the way that employees responded to them and to each other whether the office was happy or tense, formal or informal. More important, they used this information to evaluate the potential of the customer and to adjust the selling style and strategy they would use to engage the customer.

You can do the same thing on your first visit to a customer. Does the appearance of the workplace reflect a sense of order and productivity? Is it evident that people take pride in the workplace? Do the people you pass smile and say hello, or do they avoid eye contact and remain silent? When they speak, how do they sound? Are they casual and open in their interactions, or formal and reluctant to share information? What do these observations tell you about the viability of the customer?

The Financial Picture

The third facet of corporate knowledge is the financial condition of the customer's company. The customer's demand for substantiated value and the salesperson's need to become an ROI expert make the ability to understand the customer's financial picture more important than ever before in business-to-business sales. Value and ROI are always determined relative to some baseline, and in today's hypercompetitive markets, that baseline cannot be based on a hypothetical scenario or a case study from another customer. It has to be linked directly to the customer's current financial condition. Unfortunately, the financial literacy needed to accomplish this is often in short supply throughout the business world. UK-based Intellexis reported a survey that revealed that 84 percent of businesspeople are unable to correctly answer more than half of the questions in a test of basic financial knowledge.[40] Based on our 300,000 sales assessments, we estimate that roughly 80 percent of salespeople cannot read a profit-and-loss statement. The result of this shortfall is that most salespeople shy away from the quantitative and financial analysis that is becoming an increasingly important component of their work.

You can build your financial literacy in many ways. Classes in finance for non-financial professionals are among the most popular in the continuing education programs of colleges and universities, both online and off. Perhaps your company's training department already offers a class that you can attend, or you could read some of the many good books on this topic. You also could just take a member of your company's finance department to lunch for an informal discussion on the basics of corporate financial statements.

Once you have a basic understanding of finance, you can profit from the many sources of financial information regarding your prospects and customers. Annual and quarterly reports are posted on customers' Web sites and the SEC's EDGAR Database.[41] These reports contain income statements and balance sheets that will describe a customer's financial results and compare them to prior reporting periods. When you read these reports, ask yourself where the numbers come up short and what trends are visible. If you see that revenue is slowing, the customer may be eager to find solutions that can help it win more business from its own customers. If net income is shrinking, it may be a good time to offer cost savings.

Annual reports provide glimpses into the future financial concerns of the customer company, too. Companies also regularly offer projections about their future performance, which provide another valuable avenue for sales insight. The financial areas of the major search engines and portals, such as Yahoo!, MSN, and iWon.com, are another good source for these reports, as well as the projections of investment analysts, which are often more direct and frankly stated. When you read these materials, ask yourself questions such as these: What are the financial concerns that the CEO describes in the annual report's letter to shareholders? Is this company focused on revenue growth or cost cutting as it moves forward? How do analysts view the challenges that this company faces, and its future prospects? How can your solutions help?

The overall financial picture of business customers is always a strong indicator of their short-term and long-term viability as prospects and partners. It is highly unlikely that a large sale to a customer that is flirting with bankruptcy will be a profitable transaction or result in a long-term relationship. The financial picture can also offer important clues as to how likely it is that the customer will be willing to consider your solutions, how to best position those solutions to gain the customer's attention, and how long it might take before the company makes a decision to buy.

Thus far, we have been talking about understanding your customer's business from a fairly high level. World-class salespeople also need much more specific kinds of customer knowledge as they seek to sell and deliver the benefits of their solutions. We will discuss this knowledge in more detail in the customer rules in the coming chapters. For now, just be aware that this larger picture of the customer supports your ability to access and understand the specifics. It tells you whether you want to enter the customer's business, and which door might be the best access point.

CHAPTER 5

"You Must Be on Our Side"

Soon after Bill George became the CEO of Minneapolis, Minnesota–based medical devices maker Medtronic in 1991, he attended an angioplasty in which a doctor threaded one of his company's balloon catheters through the patient's arteries. As George watched, the catheter fell apart in the doctor's hands. "He was so angry," the CEO said, "that he took the catheter, covered with blood, and threw it at me. I ducked as it went sailing across the room."

After the angioplasty, George discussed the incident with one of his company's sales reps. The rep told George that he had seen the company's balloon catheters fail in exactly the same way several times before. He said he had "filed reports on the defects, but had heard nothing back." The lack of response was no longer as surprising to George and the salesperson after they calculated that the reports had to be routed through seven internal organizations within Medtronic before they ever reached the people responsible for the catheter's design. This was all "one heck of an eye-opener" to George, and he says it motivated him to institute a more customer-centric culture at Medtronic, a culture that by 2001 had helped transform it from a second-tier device maker into one of the forty most valuable companies in the United States.[42]

This is more than a story of a product failure, however; it is instructive for other reasons as well. For instance, the incident also represented a process failure. Medtronic's reporting process was obviously not working well enough to initiate a constructive resolution to what appeared to be an ongoing problem with the design of the balloon catheter. Unfortunately, this kind of process failure is not unusual. Virtually everyone who has ever called a corporation to resolve a product or service problem has a horror story to tell. Some of these have become national news, such as LaChania Govan's run-in with Comcast Cable. In 2005, she called the company more than forty times in four weeks in repeated and futile attempts to get the digital recorder that the company sold her to work properly. Finally, Comcast credited her for a month's service and sent a technician who replaced the cable box. Then, her next monthly bill arrived—with "Bitch Dog" as the addressee's name.[43]

In addition to alienating and sometimes insulting customers who are trying to report and resolve existing problems, internal company processes can also *cause* customer problems. In fact, it is estimated that sellers' systems and processes actually create approximately 25 percent of all customer problems. For example, in the 1990s, when Pepsi-Cola studied its billing process, it found errors in 44 percent of the invoices that it sent to retailers.[44] The effort and expense involved in reconciling such errors is enormous both for sellers and for their customers, to say nothing of the costs in terms of customer goodwill and long-term loyalty.

As you might expect and probably already know from direct experience, salespeople currently spend a lion's share of their time resolving errors that their companies make in the fulfillment of customer orders. Defective products, missed deliveries, picking errors and other mis-shipments, billing errors . . . the list of all of the things that can go wrong with a sale's fulfillment is seemingly endless. Given the fact that business customers expect salespeople to be their surrogate managers and single points of contact, it is no surprise that it is salespeople who get the customers' calls when things do go wrong. How much time do you spend rectifying problems like these? Over the past several decades, we have conducted a number of studies aimed at determining how salespeople spend their time. These studies have revealed that salespeople devote 50 percent to 60 percent of their time addressing customer problems that have been caused or left unresolved by their own company's policies and processes. (By the way, face-to-face selling time accounts for the least amount of salespeople's time—as little as 5 percent.)

This leads us to the third failure in the Medtronic CEO's encounter with the angry surgeon: the service failure on the part of the Medtronic salesperson. The salesperson told George that he had seen the catheters fail on several previous occasions. In filing reports on the balloon catheters, it appears that the salesperson responded as he was supposed to. But did he do what he could have, and should have, done? George does not address that question, but it might seem reasonable to conclude that if the salesperson responded according to the corporate policy, he was not at fault. Business-to-business customers, however, would *not* agree. Based on what business customers have told us, we can assure you that they would find the salesperson as culpable in their result's shortfall as both the failed product itself and the company's ineffectual reporting process.

This culpability arises because business customers expect salespeople to represent their interests. Representation means more than responding sympathetically when things do not go according to plan, more than being empathetic to the customer's plight, and more than listening "actively" to the customer's complaints. It means that, like a business agent, the salesperson actually does something in support of the customer interests. This process of acting on the customer's behalf is something the best salespeople do throughout the customer relationship.

It occurs during the sale and the delivery of the solutions, and in particular, it occurs when and where customers have the least control over the products and services that they have purchased—while they are still within the salesperson's own company. This responsibility to represent the customer's interests speaks directly to the intent of the third customer rule: *"You must be on our side."*

The Power of Customer Advocacy

How should the Medtronic salesperson have acted if he was intent on fulfilling the dictates of the third customer rule? There seem to be a number of viable options that he could have acted upon. He could have followed up on the reports to see what, if any, action had resulted. Perhaps he could have delivered the message that the company's balloon catheters were failing in the field in a more direct way, for instance, by connecting the surgeons who were experiencing the failures directly to the catheter's designer team. Maybe he should not have recommended the catheter to his customers in the first place, or should have gone so far as to steer them toward a better-quality catheter, even if it was not a Medtronic product. We can say one thing for certain: in limiting his response to the procedural requirements of his company's ineffectual reporting process and doing nothing more, the salesperson failed to fulfill the role of an effective customer advocate.

Customer advocacy is a concept on the rise in many corporations. Glen Urban, who has taught at the MIT Sloan School of Management since 1966, calls it "a major step forward in the evolving interaction between a firm and its customers."[45] He says that advocacy sits atop a pyramid that is supported by product and service quality, customer satisfaction, and relationship building. It is, however, more powerful than any of those. "This goes beyond customer focus to actively representing the customer's interests like a good friend," says Urban.[46] One reason he finds advocacy to be such a powerful concept is that it flows back and forth between buyers and sellers. Sellers serve as advocates for buyers by ensuring that customers get the results that they want. In turn, buyers serve as advocates for the seller by becoming loyal, trusting customers themselves and recommending the seller to new customers. (This reciprocity is the basis for ideas such as viral marketing, in which customers create sales momentum for companies by spreading the word about new products and services they like best.)

Urban has been studying how customer advocacy is bolstering the results of e-commerce initiatives. One example is Progressive Insurance's Web site, which informs potential customers of the best price they can get on automobile insurance, even when the best price comes from a competitor. Advocacy is not restricted to the Internet, however. It is easy to find evidence that the focus on customer advocacy is spreading throughout the corporate world. For instance, Cisco Systems was considered a pioneer when it created the position of senior vice president of customer advocacy in 1991.[47] Today, a wide range of companies, including Charles Schwab & Company, Orbitz, Sun Microsystems, and The Hartford Financial Services Group, employ executives who sport titles such as "chief customer advocate" and "director, customer experience." Their jobs are to represent the customer's point of view within their companies and to make sure that in the unending quest for efficiency and profit, companies do not forget or alienate their customers.

Customer advocacy is also the idea behind a major strategic initiative at corporate behemoth General Electric. Chairman and CEO Jeffrey Immelt is the force behind "At the Customer, For the Customer" (ACFC), which was designed to get all of the company's businesses focused on their customer's results. Under the program, GE's business units offer to help their customers improve their internal performance and results, often in areas that are completely unrelated to the products and services that GE sells them. For instance, GE Commercial Finance, which provides franchise financing for Red Robin Restaurants, sent its process experts to help the gourmet burger chain raise its on-time delivery rate for milkshakes from 36 percent to 77 percent.[48] GE Aircraft Engines helped Southwest Airlines resolve problems with another vendor's component. GE Six Sigma black belt Lori Kress, who worked with Southwest on the project, told *BusinessWeek*: "The more successful our customers are, the more successful we will be." GE is placing a large bet that this will turn out to be a business truth with a quantifiable return on investment. In 2002, it sponsored 10,000 customer projects under the auspices of ACFC.[49]

All of these occurrences—Glen Urban's positioning of advocacy as the highest level of customer interaction, the hiring of executive-level customer advocates, and GE's shift from an egocentric focus on reducing its own costs in order to maximize its profits to an external focus on the customer's well-being—are positive, early signs of a sea change in corporate thinking. As that change materializes on a large scale, it will be good news for customers and for the best business-to-business salespeople, too.

The best salespeople, according to the tens of thousands of business customers we have surveyed so far, already understand the power and the practice of customer advocacy. Unfortunately, their advocacy has often placed them at odds with their own companies. In many instances, they come to be seen as "squeaky wheels" and "rule benders" because they constantly agitate and push beyond the bounds of their authority to better serve their customers. Often, this behavior is only tolerated because these are the same salespeople who bring in the most revenue and the biggest sales.

By the way, other employees and managers within seller companies often interpret salespeople's advocacy of customers as self-serving. They think that these salespeople are protecting their own commissions at the expense of the company. Even if protecting commissions were their primary motivation, the fact remains that ensuring that their customers receive the results they have purchased, and securing long-term customer relationships in the process, creates a win/win situation rather than something that is harmful to the seller.

"There Is Only One Side in Sales," and Other Advocacy Truths

World-class salespeople share several beliefs in their quest to serve as customer advocates. They do not see sales as a zero-sum game. They eschew vested interests. They know that customer advocacy is most important when the customer is not present. These beliefs support a view of sales and selling that is customer-centric, sensible, and yet, surprisingly uncommon.

Belief #1: The Customer's Side Is the Only Side

Generally speaking, good salespeople are competitive. They want to meet and exceed their goals, outperform their competitors in the marketplace, and win the business of their customers. Every company wants a sales force composed of such people, and sales managers devote a good deal of energy to maintaining a state of high energy and motivation for this very reason. But competitiveness, like every trait, has its dark side. You always have to remain fully conscious of the fact that it has its proper limits, because when they are exceeded, competitiveness can have very negative consequences for your customers and for your company, too.

Sales competitiveness can exceed its proper limits for many reasons. The most common is probably the excessive pressure to achieve performance and revenue targets without due consideration as to how they are achieved. A salesperson's employer might impose this pressure, such as when a company pushes to "make its numbers" at the end of a quarter by focusing on the ends instead of the means. A sales manager might create this pressure by pushing a salesperson to raise his or her performance without providing the tools needed to accomplish this goal. Or salespeople might impose this pressure on themselves as they drive to earn bonuses, or perhaps to keep their jobs in the face of performance shortfalls.

SELLERS EVENTUALLY LOSE ZERO-SUM GAMES

Sellers may appear to "win" a zero-sum game in the short term, but clearly it is not a sustainable approach to profitability. Witness the not uncommon practice of channel stuffing, a zero-sum game in which companies artificially bolster their sales results by deliberately pushing more inventory on their wholesale and retail customers than those customers can possibly sell.

In 2000 and 2001, Bristol-Meyers Squibb offered its wholesalers financial incentives that amounted to "tens of millions of dollars" to buy much greater quantities of the company's pharmaceutical drugs than the market demand warranted. As a result, the drug maker's sales figures looked very healthy and the value of its stock was artificially bolstered. The problem, of course, is that selling your wholesale customers products that they cannot resell is eventually going to result in excess inventory (nearly $2 billion worth in the Bristol-Meyers Squibb case), reduced future sales, and massive returns. When the swollen wholesale inventories of the company's drugs became too large to hide, the scheme collapsed of its own weight. The Justice Department prosecuted, and shareholders initiated class-action suits. Bristol-Meyers Squibb eventually paid more than $800 million in fines and shareholder restitution. It also instituted internal controls and policies designed to ensure that the problem never recurs.[50]

No matter what the cause, when competitiveness gets out of hand, salespeople often begin treating their customers as rivals who stand between them and the attainment of their goals. In an effort to win the sale, they can become overly aggressive and/or seek to manipulate the customer. Often, they will struggle to overcome every objection, and refuse to leave without the sale. This results in the "hard sell." Almost every customer who has experienced that knows how unpleasant and unproductive it can be. The hard sell is based in a view of sales as a *zero-sum game*. In a zero-sum game, one side is going to win and one side is going to lose. This means that any gain the salesperson makes comes at cost to the customer, and vice versa. Thus, buyers and sellers end up sitting on opposite sidelines with mutually exclusive interests.

The most successful salespeople know that selling cannot be approached as a zero-sum game because there is only one winning side in a business-to-business sale—the customer's side. They know that they cannot prosper personally, and their companies cannot prosper in the long term, unless their customers prosper, too.

The reality is that if customers will not or cannot win, they will simply refuse to play a zero-sum game. Instead, they will find alternatives to your solutions and products. If you are lucky enough to have a monopoly on a product or service, the customer can, and often will, simply choose to go on living and working without it.   ·

Belief #2: You Should Beware of Vested Interests

The business news is full of stories publicizing the many ways in which vested interests can wreak havoc on customers. Suddenly, we find out that a blue-chip pharmaceutical company has hidden the side effects of a bestselling drug to maintain its profit stream, a well-respected CEO has misstated his company's earnings so that he would earn a record bonus, and a rock-solid investment analyst has rated a company's stock a "strong buy" in order to earn underwriting and other fees from the company itself.

Salespeople have vested interests, too. It is clear that their financial and career prospects are intimately linked to the performance of their companies and the sale of their company's products and services to customers. The fact that salespeople have these interests is no surprise to customers, although they are sensitive to and sometimes outright suspicious of the biases those interests can create. At the same time, customers expect and often prefer salespeople to be strong proponents of the products and services that they are selling. If salespeople are not confident of the capabilities and benefits of their company's offerings, many customers will interpret their ambivalence as a signal not to buy.

There are two problems associated with vested interests that can do irreparable harm to your ability to act as a customer advocate. The first occurs when those interests are hidden from customers. When your interests are hidden, your motives become opaque to customers and you become suspect. When customers believe that you are being less than forthright with them, they will often withhold their trust and restrict your access. Further, if customers discover hidden interests that might have influenced their thinking after the fact, they often feel betrayed and manipulated. This can create a serious crisis in the customer relationship.

Scenarios like these are actually a relatively common occurrence. Many car buyers think that the F&I managers in car dealerships who help them finance their new cars have no hidden interest in the loans, extended warranties, and services, such as undercoating, that they recommend. But when buyers learn that F&I managers earn commissions on those sales, they may see their advice in a very different, and possibly negative light. The same is true with stockbrokers. It is only natural that investors would give different consideration to a stock recommendation from a broker who stands to win a bonus or a vacation cruise for selling enough of the stock than to the same recommendation from a broker who is not earning an added bonus and perhaps not even a commission on the same sale.

The second problem caused by vested interests occurs when salespeople allow them to take precedence over the customer's best interests. Whenever salespeople are less than fully honest about their products and services, or purposely withhold knowledge that might give customers pause in the buying process, they are elevating their own interests above the customer's best interests. Often, they are also fatally underestimating their customers. Business customers are not naive; they are fully cognizant of the fact that the information and advice they receive from salespeople could be tainted by bias. They also have access to more information than ever before, and they are probably speaking to your competitors, too. In other words, the odds are that they will discover intentional lapses, and when they do, the impact on the sale and the long-term relationship with you and your company are almost always negatively impacted.

Twenty-four hundred years ago, a sharp-witted Greek playwright named Aristophanes wrote, "There is no man truly honest; we are none of us above the influence of gain."[51] It is a warning that is in keeping with the way that the best salespeople work hard to avoid conflicts of interest by being transparent and scrupulously honest. They understand that they are creating a business partnership in which each party's interest must be served, but at the same time, they make sure that their customers understand the vested interests that they have in the sale. They give their customers the appropriate opportunity to weigh the information and advice they are offering. Further, the best salespeople treat the customer's best interests as the guiding star in the sale and willingly surface and discuss any potential obstacle that might become a barrier to the customer's results, even when it is possible that those obstacles might deflect the customer away from the salespeople's solutions. In turn, their customers respond by granting these salespeople the trust and access that are prerequisites for fulfilling all of the customer rules.

Belief #3: Advocacy Is Most Valuable When the Customer Is *Not* Present

If you are of a certain age or watch reruns on television, you may be familiar with Eddie Haskell, who was a fixture on the TV series *Leave It to Beaver* in the late 1950s and early 1960s. Eddie acted like a paragon of well-behaved adolescence whenever an adult was present and just the opposite whenever he was alone with his peers. He would have been an abject failure as a customer advocate.

For all of the importance of advocacy when salespeople are face-to-face with their customers, it becomes even more critical when customers are not around. When customers are present, they are able to guard their own interests (a job often made less difficult, because just as Eddie Haskell was with adults, vendors are usually on their best behavior when they are in front of their customers). Vendors are not always so well behaved when customers are not present, when all of the internal work associated with customers' orders is being conducted. Who represents the customers' interests as their purchases are being processed, designed, manufactured, prepared for shipment, and priced within the seller's company? According to the business customers we have surveyed, the right answer should be "their salesperson."

When customers are not able to directly oversee the sale, the salesperson's ability and willingness to serve as their internal advocate and represent their interests becomes their best, and often only, protection. This is not an inconsequential job. As we have already seen, a substantial number of customer problems stem from the processes and policies of sellers. Further, regardless of the many marketing messages that promise customers that they always come first, the reality is that vendors are not making every decision and running their businesses solely with their customers' best interests in mind. Contract terms, policies, and guidelines are almost always designed to protect the vendor, not the customer. In addition, it is expensive to take into account the unique needs of each customer and make sure that each need is properly fulfilled. When sellers are faced with conflicts between keeping their businesses running as efficiently as possible and serving their customers as promised, it is the customer who often comes up short.

All of these realities make the role of the salesperson as an internal customer advocate increasingly important. The best salespeople are well aware of the need to be internal activists for their customers. They know when and how far the rules can and should be bent to the customer's advantage without creating insurmountable problems for their own companies. They are always willing to act as the customer's champion when it comes to resolving vendor disputes and problems. As our surveys reveal, their customers reward them accordingly.

The Three Skills of Customer Advocates

In addition to the proper belief system, becoming a customer advocate also requires a set of navigational, social capital, and political skills that are more important than traditional sales skills, such as cold calling and closing, when it comes to keeping customers. As we studied the capabilities of salespeople who are successful customer advocates, we found that:

- They have a thorough understanding of how their companies work, as well as the value that their customers contribute to the success of their companies.
- They have identified the internal resources they need to ensure that customers are well served, and they have cultivated and maintained extensive internal support networks.

- They tirelessly communicate their customers' expectations and needs to the managers and employees within their own companies whose actions can impact their customers' results.

Skill #1: Know Your Company

The best salespeople are as knowledgeable about the workings of their own companies as they are about the workings of their customers' companies. Their knowledge and skill at navigating their way through their companies is the foundation of their ability to expedite customer orders. They are experts at identifying and resolving customer problems, as well as preventing them in the first place. In addition to knowing how their companies operate, the best salespeople have a clear understanding of exactly what and how much their customers contribute to their company's bottom-line results. They know how to leverage the fact that a customer provides generous margins or high volume or regular repeat sales to convince their companies to act on the customer's behalf.

Internal company knowledge was instrumental in the success of paper and packaging products distributor Alling & Cory (now sold to xpedx, a division of International Paper). Regional President Tom Wolven described the ability of his salespeople like this:

> *They really get involved from one end of our business to the other. They understand credit, they understand finances, they understand shipping systems and they understand product knowledge. I think the customers really appreciate and support the salesperson who is well-rounded across all departments of our company, because at different times problems crop up in every discipline, and if he's got the knowledge of where to go and who to go to and how things work in each of those areas, and he's accessible, he's a successful sales guy.[52]*

Plainly stated, high-performing salespeople use their knowledge to manipulate the system so that it works in favor of their customers. They also use the customer's value to the company as a lever to provide added service or fast resolutions to problems. They know, for example, that a plant manager who is asked to stop production and retool a line in order to fill a special order on time is going to be far more amenable if she knows that a valuable customer relationship hinges on her decision. Sometimes, salespeople's knowledge of how their companies work enable them to stretch the system or use back channels to accomplish tasks that might not otherwise get done on time or to specification. There are almost always shortcuts in processes and procedures. The key to using them is knowing that they exist and how to access them. Other times, salespeople's internal knowledge allows them to respond proactively and sidestep problems before they occur. If, for example, you know that your company is plagued with billing errors, as Pepsi was, you can check invoices before they are sent to your customers or, better yet, help identify what causes the errors in the first place and eliminate them altogether.

A smart way to begin building your internal knowledge bank is to track the path that your customer orders travel as they move through your company. Learn about the processes and departments that your customers' orders must flow through. Locate the bottlenecks that cause delays. Identify the sources of the most common mistakes. Also, seek to identify process shortcuts. Try to discover what happens when orders are expedited, and identify where process times can be reduced in an emergency. Finally, calculate the value that each of your customers creates for your company. What are the gross sales volumes, the margins, and the ultimate profitability generated by each of your customers? Which of these individual metrics are most important to your company, and how can you use them to leverage the service that the customer receives?

PAY ATTENTION TO YOUR AMYGDALA

Oddly, some of what you know about your company may reside within your subconscious mind. The amygdala is an almond-shaped section of the brain that scientists believe helps consolidate our long-term memories and stores the emotions associated with them. It is best known as the center for fear response. If you get an uneasy feeling about a customer's order, it could be that your amygdala is responding to the clue or a combination of circumstances that have caused customer problems in the past. When you get cues like this, it pays to double-check that your customer's order is progressing as planned; sometimes premonitions about problems turn out to be accurate.[53]

Skill #2: Create Your Support Network

It is as important to know *who* makes your company work as it is to know *how* your company works. World-class salespeople create and maintain internal support networks consisting of the people who can assist them when customer problems arise. They identify the managers and employees within their companies who can help them achieve the results that their customers expect, and they make sure that they can call upon their contacts as needed. In more formal terms, they have a keen sense of the value of *social capital.*

Wayne Baker at the University of Michigan defines your social capital as all of the resources that derive from your personal and business networks. "These resources," he writes, "include information, ideas, leads, business opportunities, financial capital, power and influence, emotional support, even goodwill, trust, and cooperation." Baker maintains that individualism is a myth. He declares, "[S]ocial capital is an essential part of achieving personal success, business success, and even a happy and satisfying life."[54]

The best salespeople treat the members of their internal networks with the same care that they treat their customers. A good way to illustrate their behavior is with the story of the apocryphal salesperson who returns to his home office after a sales trip, but does not get around to meeting with his boss until the end of the day. Instead, he starts by visiting his friends in accounts receivable and the plant and the warehouse. He brightens up their days by making jokes and delivering small gifts or tickets to a ballgame. He does not appear to be working, but he is. He is thanking the members of his support network for favors they did for him while he was on the road and he is making sure that they will not have forgotten him when he calls on them in the future.

The reason the visit to the boss can wait until the end of the day is that the salesperson knows that the members of his support network are the people on whom he will depend when his customers experience the inevitable crises. He realizes that the willingness of these people to help when there are problems is determined by the quality of his personal relationship with them—the favors done and returned, the loyalty and friendship, and the occasional gift and gratuity, too.

Sometimes, a competitor might also be part of the salesperson's network. There is an oft-told story of a Hertz manager who runs out of cars and, rather than risking the loss of a loyal customer, rents a car from Avis and delivers it to the customer personally and at no charge. Next time, will the customer go to Avis because Hertz might not have a car? Of course not. He knows that one way or another Hertz will provide him with a car. If you sell a product that is a commodity and your company cannot fill an order for a valuable customer, try to obtain the product from a competitor to keep the customer happy.

Begin building your support network by identifying the people in your company who exert operational control over the processes affecting your customers' results. Make an effort to meet them and invest some time in establishing solid working relationships. Ask yourself what you can do to make their work lives a little easier. Be sure to "Go first"—that is, do something for them without the expectation of an immediate payback. Finally, show that you appreciate it when things go well. Too often, the only time managers and employees inside a company hear from salespeople is when things have gone wrong. Be doubly appreciative whenever they help you solve a customer problem.

INFLUENCING WITHOUT AUTHORITY

The best salespeople are always highly skilled influencers. After all, they cannot demand that customers buy their products and services. They must persuade customers and positively guide their decision process. The same skills that you use to influence customers come into play when you are working with an internal support network. Babson College's Allan Cohen and Stanford Graduate School of Business professor David Bradford label this ability "influence without authority" in their classic book on the subject. They say that the mindset with which you approach the members of your support network will often predetermine how effectively it operates. They suggest these four "operating rules for treating those you wish to influence":[55]

- **Mutual respect:** Always treat your network members as peers and assume that they are "competent and smart."
- **Openness:** Always be honest and "talk straight to them."
- **Trust:** Always act in the belief that your network members are as interested in supporting you as you are in supporting them.
- **Mutual benefit:** Always seek solutions that enable all of the network members involved in a situation to win.

Skill #3: Communicate Your Customer's Needs and Expectations

As a salesperson, you are a customer-facing employee. You spend all of your time thinking about and working with customers. In order to be successful, you must be very attuned to their needs and expectations. However, you should recognize that you may well be a minority within your company. Most companies are staffed with many employees who rarely, or sometimes never, come into contact with a customer. These employees do not understand your customers' business processes or the part played by the products and services they provide to your customers' companies.

This reality can become quickly and painfully clear when you examine how sellers respond to customer problems. Several decades ago, when many of the larger body parts on cars were still being made from aluminum, the Chally Group conducted a market research project for Kaiser Aluminum. During the project, one of Kaiser's major customers, a Big Three automaker, told us about an ongoing problem it was having with the car hoods supplied by our client. Kaiser was making the hoods on four huge presses in one of its plants, but one of the presses was malfunctioning, and as a result sometimes produced defective hoods. Faced with regular shipping deadlines and unable to manufacture the additional hoods needed to replace the defective pieces immediately, the operational managers at the Kaiser plant made the following command decision: They decided to always send the full shipment of hoods, including those with the defects, to the automaker in order to fulfill the terms of the contract. They reasoned that the customer would prefer to get the full shipment rather than a partial shipment, and that when the customer pulled the defective hoods, Kaiser could ship replacements in a later order.

Unfortunately, Kaiser's plant managers had no idea whether or not this was a viable solution from the customer's perspective, and they did not check with either the customer or the salesperson responsible for the account. As it turned out, the hoods were large and heavy parts, and sorting through them required a lot of space and several teams of the customer's employees. Worse, some of the defective hoods were slipping through the sorting process and causing production delays on the assembly line because nearly completed cars had to be reworked. The solution that sounded so good to Kaiser's managers was creating an ongoing crisis in the customer's assembly plant.

When we reported the story to Kaiser's sales team, they immediately solved the problem by sending a five-member employee team and a flatbed truck to the customer's plant to sort and remove the remaining defective hoods. They also created a new policy that required their company's plant managers to participate in the annual contract renewal meeting with the customer. They wanted to ensure that their managers clearly understood their customer's priorities. Soon, Kaiser earned a much larger share of the automaker's business.

The hard lesson here is that it is highly likely that many of your company's managers are not qualified to make decisions that relate to your customers. They see the world in terms of their own responsibilities and schedules, and in those terms, the right solution for your customer may not look like a viable option. For instance, operational managers will often think that it makes more sense to offer a customer a discount on the price to make up for a missed shipment than it does to manufacture and ship several partial shipments. Unfortunately, a few dollars saved is not going to be much consolation to a customer who has to shut down his lines because of the missing parts.

The proactive solution to problems like these is education. The best salespeople make sure that the managers and employees within their companies understand the customer's needs and expectations. You can begin this process of education by anticipating the problems that might arise as your customer's order is processed. Ask yourself—or better yet, subtly ask your customers—what kinds of resolutions would work best for

---

Five Ways to Become a Better Expediter

1. Network with all key internal people before problems arise.
2. Build rapport with every key function, and develop as many working friendships as possible.
3. Visit key function areas to learn how they work.
4. Personally credit others for their assistance, and make sure they hear good news as well as bad news.
5. Identify the "higher authorities" to contact if standard resolution methods are not sufficient.

---

them. Ask your company's managers how they would normally address common customer problems. Then, make sure their solutions are aligned to your customer's needs. Further, when customers have special needs and expectations, make sure that everyone involved with fulfilling the order is aware of them. Finally, make sure that you will be a participant in the resolution of problems. You want to be part of the decision-making process, not surprised by it.

The Platform of Professional Competence

In the previous three chapters, we have explored the first three rules that business customers expect salespeople to abide by. We have seen how and why world-class salespeople act as business agents and accept accountability for their customers' results. We have seen how and why they develop and demonstrate their understanding of their customers' businesses by analyzing them with a CEO's eyes. Finally, we have seen how and why they position themselves on the customer's side of the table by representing and protecting the customer's best interests as advocates and expediters.

These three rules and their associated skills are the cornerstones of an elevated platform of professional competence. This platform enables salespeople to stand above a large majority of their competitors. More important, it allows them to stand out in their customers' minds as attractive business partners. Now, it is time to build upon that platform in the quest to supercharge your performance and achieve sales excellence.

The Advanced Rules of Sales Excellence

You do not sell in a vacuum. Your customers' needs, your company's offerings and targets, and the competitive challenges you face are always changing and making ever-increasing demands on you. The three rules of professional competence described in Part Two provide the basis for meeting those demands and building a strong foundation for your sales success. But what happens when you are competing against another salesperson with the same foundational level of skills or when, as will eventually be the case, the majority of salespeople all have the same skill level? The four rules of Part Three, which we call the advanced rules of sales excellence, offer a solution to those dilemmas.

The four advanced rules and their associated skills are refinements and extensions of the foundational rules. In other words, they cannot and should not be thought of as discrete skills. If you are not accountable for customer results, do not understand the customer's business, and do not act as your customer's advocate, you cannot fulfill the customer demands that underlie the second set of rules or effectively wield the skills that derive from them.

Once you have mastered the skills of the first three rules, however, the second set of rules will enable you to raise your performance and success to the pinnacle of sales success. This is a rarified position. In our surveys, business customers have awarded it to fewer than 1 percent of the salespeople with which they come into contact. It is also a privileged position. Business customers award the largest share of their business to these world-class salespeople.

As with the previous rules, the final four customer rules are *not* based on the subjective opinions of business customers, which are usually skewed by their most recent or most vivid experiences and/or the desire to please the interviewer. Instead, they are derived from and correlated against business customers' buying habits. These results empirically prove that when customers make their buying decisions, they place substantial weight on these final four expectations of salespeople:

First, they expect salespeople to understand that the feature and benefit attributes of their products and services are only inert descriptions of value. Descriptions of features and benefits cannot tell customers how to apply the solutions, and they do not help customers in their quest to actually capture the results they hope to achieve. Instead, customers want salespeople who are experts in the practical applications of their offerings and who are able to explain how the customer's people, processes, and technologies will have to adjust in order to implement and capture solution value.

Second, they expect salespeople to realize that one of the most stressful aspects of working with any outsourced business partner is the limited accessibility that the customer has to the vendor's staff and resources. Customers want to work with salespeople who will respond immediately to their calls for assistance and who will provide them with the service they need whenever and wherever it is required.

Third, they expect salespeople to recognize that problems will inevitably arise over the course of any sustained business relationship. Customers want to work with salespeople who are able to proactively identify, consider, and discuss the problems that tend to occur in the purchase, delivery, and use of their products and services. (They cannot and will not buy from salespeople who ignore or hide the potential barriers to their desired results.) Further, customers demand that salespeople constructively address their problems by either personally resolving them or by assembling and supervising the specialists who can.

Fourth, they expect salespeople to know that in free markets the challenges of competition and change are always present, and that those businesses that are not growing are dying. Accordingly, customers want to work with salespeople who are prepared to provide new and added value to their businesses on a continuous basis. These are salespeople who can recognize and respond to their customer's spoken and unspoken needs with the incremental and breakthrough improvements that are capable of driving the customer's results to new and higher levels.

The four advanced rules described in the chapters of Part Three encapsulate and clarify these customer expectations. Their associated skills are designed to enable you to improve your ability to establish, retain, and expand your business with new and existing customers. The next four chapters will describe how you can demonstrate and persuade your customers of the applicability of your products and services, your accessibility, your problem-solving prowess, and your ability to deliver innovations that will create new value for their companies. These are the rules and the skills that will help you win new customers when the competition is at its most intense, and enable you to create the levels of loyalty and sales growth that mark the most profitable relationships with existing customers.

CHAPTER 6

"You Must Bring Us Applications"

It is unusual to find a salesperson profiled in a business magazine. It is much rarer to find such a profile in *The New Yorker*, a literary magazine covering contemporary culture. Then, one of its writers, James Stewart, went to Steinway Hall, the venerable piano maker's flagship showroom in Manhattan, and met Erica Feidner, who, in 2001, had been Steinway & Sons' top salesperson for six years running. She sold $4 million worth of pianos in 1999.

Feidner's success derived from her ability to match potential buyers to pianos. Her *New Yorker* profile "Matchmaker" (August 20, 2001) opens with a description of how after a discussion with a new customer, Feidner writes a number on a slip of paper. She then leads the customer through the 300-odd pianos on display, the largest inventory of Steinways in the world. The customer plays more than a dozen, but is unable to find one that is exactly right. Feidner mentions that there is a new arrival, which she has played, but it is not yet on the floor. The piano is brought to the display floor and, while playing it, the customer quickly realizes it is perfect. Feidner produces the piece of paper on which she had written the number earlier in the day. The number matches the serial number of the piano the customer has decided to buy.

Magic? It certainly feels that way to many of the customers who purposely seek out Feidner when they shop for a Steinway. But as Stewart delves into her methods, another picture emerges. For instance, at the beginning of a sale, Feidner habitually spends an hour or more chatting with the customer—not about the heritage, quality, or available models and options of Steinway's pianos, but about the customer's level of play, playing style, taste in music, where and how often the customer will play the piano, what he or she will play on it, and what kind of response, action, and tone the customer expects.

Although she was trained as a professional pianist and can make a piano sing, Feidner insists that her customers play the pianos they are considering rather than having her play for them. She leaves audience-shy customers alone while they play. If she is working with neophytes or non-players who are buying for someone else, she teaches them how to hear, feel, and describe the differences in pianos, and she teaches them simple tunes so that they can play, too. Stewart, who was planning to buy a Yamaha piano before meeting Feidner and eventually purchased a Steinway for twice the price instead, writes:

> [A]fter they meet her many soon find themselves in the grip of musical ambitions they never knew they harbored. These ambitions often include buying a specific piano that they feel they can no longer live without, even if it strains both their living rooms and their bank accounts.

Interestingly, Steinway's best salesperson for years running does not always have the company's highest closing ratio with walk-in customers. One of the reasons is that she does not push her customers into buying decisions. Stewart himself "forgets" he is on a selling floor as he makes repeated visits to Steinway Hall to play the pianos, until he is startled to discover that one that he liked has been sold to someone else. Another reason is that Feidner is driven to sell each of her customers the perfect piano. "She will often ask a customer to wait until the right piano materializes, and this can take months or, in rare cases, years," writes Stewart.

Luckily, Feidner does not need to close sales quickly to maintain her sales volume. Instead, she spends a substantial portion of her time maintaining contact with and providing service to her existing customers. For instance, she encourages Stewart to take lessons to improve his playing skills and recommends three teachers, one of whom he finds is a "good match." (Feidner has worked with more than 800 teachers in the New York City area, many of whom refer potential customers.) She invites him to attend recitals at Steinway Hall. She even asks him to play in one. After Stewart accepts, and while he is traveling on a book tour, Feidner helps him maintain his practice schedule by arranging for him to play Steinways in each city he visits. Stewart ranks his appearance at the recital "among the high points of my life."

As a result of services like these, Feidner is able to maintain her flow of deals through referrals from her customers. (*The New Yorker* article is essentially a 7,000-word customer recommendation read by three-quarters of a million subscribers.) In fact, the stream of recommendations she receives is so robust that in June 2004, Feidner was able to tell *Inc.* magazine, which featured her on the cover, that she was only seeing new customers by referral.[56]

How does Feidner's highly successful selling strategy relate to the business-to-business environment? Let's review its major elements:

- The salesperson has expert knowledge of the product.
- The sales process is intensely focused on the customer's needs and the intended use of the product being purchased.
- The process includes the education and guidance that the customer requires to make the best buying decision.
- The salesperson refuses to sell a product that will not fulfill the customer's needs.

- The salesperson treats the sale itself as the first step in an ongoing process designed to ensure that the customer receives all of the benefits of the purchase.

These elements all sound very familiar to us because they are the same qualities that we hear business customers describing. These are qualities that the customers we have studied consistently identify with the world-class salespeople. They are also the qualities that satisfy the customer expectations and demands that have given rise to the fourth customer rule: *You must bring us applications.*

Applications Trump Features and Benefits

If you think back to the three overarching customer "wants" that we discussed in Chapter 2, it is clear that each is intimately connected to the fourth customer rule, which requires that salespeople provide applications. First, customers want *substantiated value*, a demand that cannot be fulfilled until whatever you are selling has been successfully applied. It must be in place and producing results. Second, they want *solutions* rather than products and services. In other words, they do not want to hear a soliloquy on features and benefits, no matter how entertaining. They want to learn how the offering fits their needs, see that it can be implemented, and be convinced that it will produce the results they desire. Third, they want to *outsource* any element of their business that is not a core competence. In other words, they will almost always want you to take on as much of the implementation of the solution, and the ongoing management responsibility for it, as is feasible.

These are the major reasons why a focus on solution applications will virtually always trump recitations of features and benefits—no matter how compelling they may be—in today's business-to-business environment. Your customers know that if they cannot capture the promise of value through successful application, the return they can earn on their investment will be, at best, limited and at worst, a total loss that might also negatively impact other aspects of their business performance and corporate results. The latter case is not an exaggeration. Consider, for example, what can happen to a company's productivity and workflow when the implementation of an enterprise-wide IT package runs off the rails.

The more complex the solutions you sell, the more critical and the more valuable your application expertise becomes to your customers. Pianos are not often thought of as complex products, but unlike many mass-produced instruments, there are substantial differences between each of Steinway's handmade pianos. Every piano that Erica Feidner sells responds differently when played, and every one has a unique sound. Every customer to whom she sells has a different repertoire and playing style. It is no wonder that customers place a high premium on her ability to create the perfect match between piano and player. The same is true of any complex business solution. Your ability to create the perfect match between your offerings and your customers' situations is a critical skill in bringing them applications.

At first glance, products and services that are commodities might not appear to require the same degree of application expertise on the part of salespeople as do more complex products. Commodities are typically mature, standardized categories of products and services with which customers are already very familiar. Accordingly, it is often suggested that customers do not need salespeople to provide applications in order to buy the commodities, use them, and achieve the desired results. Surprisingly, however, our studies of business customers have revealed just the opposite. Buyers in commodity markets consider application expertise to be as valuable, if not more valuable, than do buyers of complex solutions.

While the *need* for application expertise might not be as great in commodity markets, its relative rarity makes it an added benefit and a strong differentiating factor. Further, while commodities themselves may not be unique, the customers that buy them are. Each of your business customers has a unique strategy, culture, business structure, and so on. Each has different needs and is driving toward different results. Because of all these customer-based variables, the ways in which commoditized products and services can be applied within individual companies are unique too. The salesperson's ability to bring applications to commodity customers can improve their customers' results. Thus, salespeople who can provide application expertise shine in their customers' eyes.

In fact, as you can see in the table that follows, almost all of the sales forces rated world class by the business customers in our studies have been sellers of products that are usually considered low-margin commodities in mature markets, such as printing

---

CONSULTATIVE SELLING

The idea of salespeople as consultants should be familiar to anyone who has been following the evolution of sales strategy. Mack Hanan, along with coauthors James Cribbin and Herman Heiser, first coined the phrase "consultative selling" in a book of the same name published by the American Management Association in 1970. It has proven to be a perennially popular concept. Hanan's substantially heftier seventh edition of the book was published in 2004.

The original edition proposed consultative selling as a solution for key account selling in a newly emerging business environment that the authors characterized as driven by "increased product standardization," "accelerated competition," "protracted price erosion," "demands for customer service," and "stratified decision making."[57] If you compare this list to your sales challenges today, it suggests that there might be some truth in the old quote, "The more things change, the more they remain the same."

paper, business forms, office supplies, chemicals, and original equipment auto parts. Only two companies have been identified as world-class more than once, and they are in commodity markets, too. Because everything else is more or less equal in these industries, capabilities such as the application expertise of salespeople have an oversized impact on the customer.

How Customers Rank Selling Effectiveness in Different Industry Segments

Rank	Industry	Average Rating
1	Fine Paper	89.50
2	Business Forms	88.65
3	Maintenance, Repair, and Operations	88.47
4	Original Equipment Auto Parts	88.36
5	Office Supplies	88.27
6	Chemicals	87.97
7	Rubber	87.87
8	Primary Metals	87.74
9	Electronics	87.70
10	Office Productivity	86.67
11	Aftermarket Auto Parts	86.52
12	Health Care	86.10
13	Pharmaceuticals	85.99
14	Computers and Software	85.80
15	Delivery/Freight*	85.51
16	Telecommunications	82.54

*Freight combined with Mail into a "Delivery" segment

Key to Ratings:
100 = Excellent
 90 = Very Good
 80 = Good
 70 = Average
 60 = Poor

Whether you sell complex solutions or commodities, providing applications requires a very different approach than presenting features and benefits. The primary expertise of salespeople who focus on features and benefits is product (and/or service) knowledge. This knowledge becomes the basis for describing the attributes of their products and services, as well as the generic benefits that those attributes can deliver to the customer. The ability to successfully provide applications requires product knowledge, too, but that is not enough. It also requires extended application competence, such as understanding customers' needs and installation and integration considerations. This is why we say that world-class salespeople adopt the role of the *consultant* in order to fulfill the fourth customer rule.

The Salesperson as Consultant

There are many reasons why the consultant metaphor is applicable to the work of providing applications. Consultants are expected to understand their clients' wants and needs. They are expected to provide expert, objective advice on how to best address those wants and needs. Often, they are engaged to manage the implementation of the solutions they recommend, as well as integrating them into the client's existing business systems. Finally, consultants are also increasingly being called upon to ensure that the solutions continue to produce the desired results as long as they are in use. (It is only a small step from this last consulting service to outsourcing, which is the primary reason so many of the biggest players in the global consulting industry have also become major providers of outsourced services.) These are the same tasks that we see business customers demanding of salespeople. Not coincidentally, they are also tasks that are integral to the customer-centered sales strategies that so many business-to-business sellers have adopted.

As with any metaphor, there are some limits to the consultant role that salespeople should keep in mind. Consultants are paid for the time they spend with clients, but salespeople (and/or the companies that employ them) are paid only if and when a sale materializes. Second, consultants are paid no matter which solutions they recommend to their clients, but salespeople are rewarded for providing the fixed set of solutions offered by their companies. In other words, there are times when the roles of the salesperson and the consultant rightfully diverge.

When salespeople forget or confuse these distinctions, they sometimes end up becoming what Prime Resource Group founder Jeff Thull calls "unpaid consultants." They can also become what George Dudley of Behavioral Sciences Research Press terms "professional visitors."[58] The best salespeople avoid these pitfalls by remaining focused on the fact that to be successful they must sell their products and services. This does not mean that they sell inappropriate solutions to their customers; rather, it means that they quickly and continuously evaluate the fit between their customers' needs and the salesperson's solutions. Whenever it becomes clear that resolving a customer's problem cannot serve both the customer and the salesperson's company, these salespeople move to more viable opportunities.

That said, a good way to understand the work of providing applications is to think of your sales in terms of four levels of application competence and accountability:

1. The first level of competence encompasses the *specification*, or the proper configuration of the application.
2. The second level of competence is the delivery and *installation* of the application.
3. The third level of competence is the *integration* of the application into the customer's existing business system.
4. The fourth level of competence is the *usage* or ongoing delivery of the application's desired results, as well as the identification of the customer's future needs.

Sometimes salespeople will have the competence needed to fulfill each application level on their own. Sometimes they will call upon and supervise a team of application experts who will assist them in providing the information and expertise needed to fulfill the dictates of each level. In every case, and in keeping with the first customer rule, world-class salespeople always take on accountability for the successful completion of each level.

Let's take a look at the components of each of these levels, the responsibilities that business customers expect salespeople (and their teams) to shoulder in each, and the skills that salespeople need to employ to fulfill those responsibilities.

Level One: Specification Competence

The first level of application competence and accountability is the specification of the best solution to the customer's problem. This is the challenge described by Cindy Shulman, sales manager in Exxon Chemical's Polypropylene Division, during a Selling Power–sponsored roundtable conference with winners of Chally's World-Class Sales Excellence Award:

> *Salespeople must be able to understand their customers' needs in terms of where they want to go. They must figure out how to match up our capabilities with the customer's needs and how to bring organization to the customer's goals. . . . Salespeople must understand what the customer really wants and be able to develop win/win solutions.*[59]

As Shulman says, "win/win solutions" are built around the fit between the seller's capabilities and the customer's needs. To analyze and create that fit, salespeople cultivate two basic types of knowledge: knowledge of their products and services, as we mentioned earlier, and knowledge of the customer's unique situation and condition. Both are critical prerequisites of "fit."

Knowledge Type #1: Applied Product Knowledge

Most customer-centered sales processes begin with an analysis of customer needs, but customer needs are *not* the true starting point for specification competence. Before salespeople contact prospective customers, they must know what they are selling and, in particular, the capabilities their companies can deliver to customers. The best salespeople filter everything that their customers tell them about their needs and wants through this prism of product and service capabilities, looking for the points of intersection. They know that this is the acid test of applicability. If a salesperson contacts a customer who has a problem that his company's solutions cannot address in a significant way, it is a disservice to the customer and waste of the salesperson's time to continue through the sales process.

Product knowledge is relatively common among business-to-business salespeople. Most sellers provide product knowledge training as a component in the orientation of new salespeople. They also train their sales forces when new products and services are launched as part of the process of bringing them to market. Many sellers, however, remain more focused on product features than on the solution capabilities that can be derived from those features. Furthermore, a significant number of sellers do not provide any product knowledge training to their employees—19.4 percent in 2005, according to *Training* magazine.[60] If your employer is among the former, you will need to translate product features into capabilities. If your employer is among the latter, you will have to develop your applied product knowledge on your own. In any case, the best salespeople have a well-developed comprehension of both the features and capabilities of their products and services. They are also well aware of the practical limitations of their knowledge, and they do not "stretch" those limits. Instead, they know when to call in expert help from within their companies, and they know whom to call in, too.

Knowledge Type #2: Granular Customer Knowledge

The second prerequisite of "fit" is knowledge of the customer's situation and/or problems. We have already described the importance of understanding the customer's business in the macro sense of the CEO in Chapter 4, but when it comes to applications, the salesperson's understanding has to take a sharper focus. Salespeople need information that is more granular and practical in order to provide the right application. This is usually operational information that is directly related to the solution capabilities that they are selling. The only sources for it are direct observation and/or the employees within the customer company.

This is where needs analysis and other information-gathering tools and skills become an integral part of the sales process. There are three reasons that understanding the intricacies of the customer's situation in detail is critical to sales success:

- **First,** you cannot solve a problem you do not understand. If you do not know what conditions and situations the customer is experiencing, you cannot determine the appropriate solutions.
- **Second,** you cannot set a goal without a baseline. If you do not understand the customer's current position, you cannot determine whether your product or service has delivered any benefit to the customer.
- **Third,** you cannot sell a solution to a customer who does not recognize that he has a problem. If your customers do not realize that they are experiencing "pain," they have no reason to buy your applications.

It is for all of these reasons that the best salespeople become experts at uncovering the full dimensions of their customers' problems. Most important, they know how to create the customer trust and gain the access to the customer's organization that are required to glean information about the customer's condition. They know where to go within a customer's company to discover the problems that their products and services address. Once they reach those locations, they know how to elicit the information they need. They are expert questioners, and they know how to listen and what to listen for in the answers that customers give.

Isabel Kersen, past president of the Professional Society for Sales & Marketing Training, summed up all of these skills well when she said, "Salespeople need to understand the customer's real needs and make the right connection with the company's solutions. If they are not good at learning, they won't be able to connect the two. The most important thing we can teach salespeople is how to learn all the time."[61]

The best salespeople complete the specification process by comparing what they have learned about the customer's needs to the capabilities offered by their companies. They know how

---

ATTRIBUTES THAT SUPPORT SPECIFICATION COMPETENCE

Salespeople who are experts at specifying applications generally are able to:

- Develop a sound understanding of applications in order to quickly assess a sales opportunity and prioritize how much time to devote to it.
- Understand customer needs in order to properly configure an application with the appropriate group of features and options.
- Focus on the intangible and emotional benefits that will ensure customer satisfaction, as well as provide the rationale that justifies the purchase.
- Vary the benefit message to fit the buyer even when the product offering is fairly fixed.

---

to match problems and solutions and create the best fit. Finally, they are experts at communicating applications to the decision-makers within their customers' companies. They do this by not only describing the proposed application, but by describing the conditions that justify its use and the benefits that will accrue to their customers as those conditions are successfully addressed. In other words, they walk their customers through the specification process.

Level Two: Installation Competence

Specifying the right solution is essential, but until that solution is in place and ready to use, it is useless to your customers. That brings us to the second level of knowledge that salespeople must develop—installation competence. Salespeople with installation accountability ensure that the products and services they are selling can be, and are, *delivered* and *implemented* as agreed.

Delivery means that the right goods and services appear at the right place in the right time frame. It sounds simple and it should be, but answer this: how many times have you stopped doing business with a company because you received the wrong merchandise, or you did not receive what you ordered at all, or you received it before you were ready for it or after you expected it? The reality is that minor mistakes can kill customer relationships just as easily as do major problems. In fact, they actually kill more business relationships, because they occur much more frequently.

Implementation means that the product is set up and ready to use or that the service is in place and ready to execute. Machinery must be unpacked, assembled, and tested; software has to be installed; employee data must be obtained and uploaded. In this case, the salesperson takes responsibility for ensuring that the customers can begin using the application in the time frame specified in the contract.

The degree of installation competence you need to attain will vary widely depending on what you sell. You will always have delivery considerations. At Chally, we administer assessments over the Internet, but we must still "deliver" remote access to our databases to our clients so that they can take our tests, read test results, and utilize the variety of other services we offer. It is possible that you might be selling in an environment that does not have implementation considerations, such as selling paper to customers who will load it into a printer themselves. But every day, there are fewer and fewer of these "drop at the dock" sales that involve salespeople. Already, the vast majority of them are either automated and transmitted over the Internet or taken over the phone by customer service reps in call centers.

When we study world-class salespeople, we find that the following three tasks (and skill sets) are associated with installation competence.

Scheduling: The best salespeople are expert schedulers. They do not passively accept deadlines, nor do they agree to installation terms their companies cannot meet. Instead, they are realistic in the establishment of the timing for application delivery and implementation. They work with their customers to define the installation expectations for the application. They create installation timelines and surface timing conflicts by working backward from the date that the customer requires the application to be in place and ready to use. They ensure that their companies can meet the proposed timeline. In addition, they communicate the resulting schedule to everyone who will be responsible for meeting the dates agreed upon.

Coordination: The best salespeople are expert coordinators. They proactively manage the interaction of all of the parties involved in the sale. They make sure that their own companies' employees, outside contractors, and their customers' employees are properly introduced and are aware of each other's responsibilities and needs. These salespeople pay specific attention to the handoff points in the delivery and implementation of their applications. They know that these points often represent "white spaces" between functions and organizations, a sort of no man's land where neither party has full responsibility for or total control of the application, and each assumes the other is managing the process.

Confirmation: Finally, the best salespeople avoid unpleasant surprises by confirming, as opposed to assuming, that deadlines have been met. They check to make sure that the applications they sell are moving through the installation timeline as expected. They follow up within their organizations to ensure that production and processing deadlines are kept. They confirm shipping dates and track orders to make sure that deliveries are made. They call their customers to make sure that shipments have arrived and contain everything that they should. They confirm dates with installers and check to ensure that everything needed to implement the application will be available. And finally, they contact or meet with their customers to confirm that the application is in place and ready to use.

Level Three: Integration Competence

If you are past a certain age it will not seem so long ago that a copier was a monster of a machine that was usually only leased from its real master. Its inner workings were arcane and its output was fickle. The installation of this beast was relatively simple, but that did not guarantee that you would receive its full benefits. You had to be prepared to receive the copier, which needed a proper office and certain climatic conditions. Someone, a so-called "key holder," had to be taught how to feed and coddle it. These were considerations that were part and parcel of the third level of application knowledge—integration competence.

Integration competence and accountability is critical because the installation of your solutions is never enough to ensure that the customer will receive their full benefit. Your solutions must also be aligned with all of the elements already in place within the customer's company. You will find that the importance of the distinction between installation and integration tends to rise in tandem with the complexity of your application.

There are many examples of solutions that require integration. SFA (sales force automation) is one that might be very familiar to you. When SFA solutions were first introduced, many of the companies that purchased and installed them had a difficult time realizing the increases in sales productivity and customer service and satisfaction that SFA vendors were trumpeting at every opportunity. There were several reasons for these shortfalls in benefit achievement. For one, the customers' sales forces first had to be trained to use the software, and then had to change their behaviors and routines to accommodate it. For another, other functions within the companies, such as customer service and support, had to be able to easily access the relevant customer data that was collected by the new SFA systems. The SFA software had to be seamlessly integrated with the companies' legacy systems. One or both of these integration requirements were often less than comprehensively addressed by SFA sellers, and as a result, many early SFA projects were deemed failures.

Integration challenges, like those inherent in SFA, often spell the difference between a handsome return on investment and none at all. They are also challenges that are very difficult for customers to identify in advance. Further, many salespeople tend to downplay or even purposely ignore them, especially when they think that the integration barriers might scare off the customer. This is a serious mistake; these salespeople quickly discover that they cannot attain sales success unless their customers attain the results they expect. That is why world-class salespeople accept a full measure of integration accountability.

In taking accountability for the integration of applications, salespeople consider the customers' existing business system.

The best salespeople ensure that their applications are properly integrated into their customers' business by seeking to understand the impact of their applications, preparing their customers for the issues that normally arise in application adoption, and ensuring that those issues are properly addressed.

The skills that world-class salespeople use to bolster their integration competence are essentially change management skills. The integration of any new application entails changes in the customer's business system. Accordingly, world-class salespeople prepare their customers to attain the full benefit of their solutions by anticipating the impacts that their applications will create and the changes they will require as they are woven into the following three elements of the customer's business system.

People: Anytime your products and services require the support and participation of the customer's employees, you must consider the human issues of change. The best salespeople recognize that many people dislike change, and some actively resist it. They also understand that the behavioral changes that their customer's employees must make to use new applications are often the most difficult to achieve. So, they assess the customer's culture and working mores, surface any conflicts between current practices and those required for the new application, and offer their customers strategies that will help them successfully navigate any required changes.

The best salespeople also ensure that customers understand the degree and content of employee training required to successfully utilize their applications. They arrange for the necessary training, and then confirm that the customer's employees have actually learned everything they need to know to use the application.

Process: One way to view a business is as a collection of processes that are aligned and work together to create added-value products and services. Everything that a business customer buys is somehow related to these processes. It might be consumed by,

ARE YOU ON-BOARDING YOUR CUSTOMERS?

On-boarding is traditionally thought of as a human resources strategy for processing and orienting new employees, but in recent years, an increasing number of companies have been applying the concept to new customers. These companies pay extra attention to their customers during the first 90 to 120 days, a "honeymoon" period during which the customers are usually most open to communication. During that period, sellers who have adopted on-boarding strategies contact the customers more frequently, collect information that enables them to better know and serve their new customers, and craft offers that increase satisfaction, loyalty, and new sales, too. On-boarding has proven to be especially effective at lowering the attrition rates early in the customer relationship in sectors such as banking and telecommunications.

added to, or become a component of one or more processes. In other words, everything you sell has process ramifications; it must mesh properly with the customer's existing processes.

The best salespeople understand the workings and requirements of processes with which their applications interact. If they sell consumables or raw materials, such as paper, fuel, or chemicals, they know what capabilities the process must have and how it must operate to make proper use of their products. If they sell goods or services that are intended to become a component within a process, they investigate how it will impact the operation of other components in the process, and what adjustments have to be made to the application or the existing process to ensure that they are properly aligned.

Technology: The final element of a business system encompasses the technologies that power and speed its processes and empower its people. In the modern company, these are usually information technology systems that control processes, deliver information on demand, and automate work that was previously done manually. To be effective and deliver their full benefit, the product and service applications that you bring to your customers must also be aligned to and work with the existing technologies.

The best salespeople are experts at recognizing the potential conflicts that exist between their solutions and their customers' technologies. They know how to determine whether or not the standards and architecture of technologies used by their customers are compatible with the applications they are proposing. This is not to say that they can personally resolve all these issues, which often require the specialized knowledge of applications engineers of all ilks. Rather, they know enough to realize whether and where problems may exist and are able to call in the resources needed to address them before compatibility conflicts occur.

Level Four: Usage Competence

Once your products and services are specified, installed, and integrated within the customer's business, there is one last set of application considerations that the best salespeople seek to understand and manage. This final level of competence encompasses all of the ongoing service requirements that ensure that the application will continue to deliver all of the customer's desired outcomes. This level is *usage competence.*

Virtually every product and service has one or more usage issues and corresponding opportunities, including those that follow.

Replacement: If you sell a product that is consumed, eventually it will have to be replaced. Its inventory levels must be maintained, and it must be restocked in a regular and timely manner. Salespeople and companies that accept accountability in this area enjoy high levels of customer loyalty. Often, we see them develop into experts at the replacement process. For instance, they might provide automated replenishment services that guarantee that the customer always has the optimal inventory levels on hand, while simultaneously minimizing the customer's costs with just-in-time delivery. In bundling simple commodities with added-value services such as these, salespeople create a continual stream of repeat sales.

Maintenance: If you sell a product that executes an operation, its usage requirements probably include periodic maintenance, fuel or other fluids, and replacement parts. Again, the opportunity to create and sell added-value services is present. Service contracts, leases, aftermarket parts manufacturing and sales, and outsourced maintenance services are all huge business sectors that have grown out of sellers' attention to maintenance considerations.

Updates: If you sell software, Internet services, data, or one of the many products and services associated with the digital age, the usage requirements of your applications are likely to include periodic updates that must be delivered and installed to keep the application working properly, as well as patches designed to repair newly discovered flaws or security exposures. We are just starting see the myriad opportunities for new sales that these usage factors are generating. The success of Salesforce. com is a good example. It created a hosted SFA solution that eliminated much of the time, effort, and stress that business customers were experiencing when they purchased off-the-shelf or custom SFA packages, and it was handsomely rewarded by customers and investors.

In their rush to win new business, shortsighted salespeople often sidestep the usage requirements of their applications or leave their fulfillment to other people. They mistakenly see this as the rote responsibility of their company's service and support staff. In taking this view, however, they risk losing customers to neglect, errors, or, even worse, the attentions of more application-savvy competitors. Further, they miss valuable opportunities to strengthen the customer relationship, earn the customer's loyalty, and win repeat business.

By not focusing on usage needs and how they change over time, these salespeople also miss an important opportunity to identify and fulfill the future needs of their customers, a topic that we will discuss at length in Chapter 9. Perhaps because they are too focused on new business or short-term challenges that leave them little time to think strategically, or because they do not maintain ongoing contact with the customer, they are unable to see coming needs that customers have not yet recognized and thus provide solutions that could meet them.

The ability to anticipate the customer's future needs is an advanced level of usage competence that enables the best salespeople to earn access to the C-level (that is, "chief" or top-level) decision-makers in customer companies regardless of the nature of the product or service they provide. For this reason as well as the others already described, world-class salespeople develop their expertise in the usage requirements of their applications and take every opportunity to fulfill those ongoing customer needs themselves.

The four levels of application competence and accountability—specification, application, integration, and usage—are the key to satisfying the dictates of the fourth customer rule. If you can meet and exceed the expectations of business customers in this regard, they will be able to see beyond the features and benefits of the products and services you sell and consider them in their true light as a means for reaching their business goals. No matter what you sell, if you remain focused on fulfilling the fourth customer rule, you can raise the level of your game and increase your share of your customers' business.

CHAPTER 7

"You Must Be Easily Accessible"

I n November 2005, American Airlines launched "Keeping Up with Jenkins," an advertising campaign featuring a hard-working, fast-moving road warrior. In the TV commercial, an executive strides through an office filled with cubicles. "Jenkins . . . Jenkins," he calls out before asking the nearest employee, "Do you know where Jenkins sits?"

"Sir, Jenkins doesn't actually work here," she hesitantly answers.

"But he's around here all the time. I saw him this morning," protests the executive.

"Yeah, he's our software supplier from Chicago," says the woman. Several of her nearby coworkers nod confirmation.

The commercial cuts away to Jenkins at the airport, but it returns to the office for the punch line, where the bemused executive, walking away, mutters to himself, "I was going to give him a raise."[62]

American Airlines obviously realizes that clueless bosses are always good for a chuckle, but it also knows something about what makes salespeople successful. It is clear that Jenkins is acting as a surrogate manager. He is effective enough in this role that the executive has trouble believing that Jenkins is not one of his company's employees. Of course, the airline is promoting itself as the enabler of the fictional salesperson's performance, but it is flying right when it suggests that your accessibility to customers is a major factor in your sales success.

The problem is that the average salesperson spends an astonishingly small percentage of his or her time in direct contact with customers. In fact, studies typically reveal that administrative chores and traveling eat up the two largest chunks of salespeople's working lives. As mentioned in Chapter 5, the work behavior studies we have conducted found that salespeople spend only 5 percent of their time selling face-to-face with customers. Salespeople themselves are surprised by this figure. They typically estimate that they spend much more time with their customers. Proudfoot Consulting reports similar results in its annual studies of corporate productivity, which are based on what it discovers at its client companies. In the latest, it found that salespeople spend only 11 percent of their time actively selling.[63]

We can safely assume that salespeople *do* spend additional time in direct contact with customers, which is sales-related, if not selling per se. Proudfoot reported that its clients' sales forces spent 14 percent of their time problem-solving and 10 percent of their time prospecting, both of which would logically include some direct contact with customers. But even if that doubles or triples the total amount of contact, salespeople are still spending the majority of their time on tasks that do not include their customers—and business customers are not happy about it.

It is actually quite ironic. Salespeople are generally eager to spend time with prospective customers, who are often busily avoiding them. On the other hand, salespeople generally neglect their existing customers, who want to spend more time with them. We know this based on the results of the many proprietary, industry-specific market research studies we have conducted for our corporate clients. In each, we ask business-to-business customers questions about the contact rate of the salespeople from their existing vendors, such as "How often do you expect to be visited?" and "How often do you expect to be called?" When we compare their expectations to the number of sales visits and calls they receive, the actual contact levels almost invariably come up short.

This is particularly troublesome because this personal contact is a major factor in retaining customers and expanding existing sales relationships, two activities that make an oversized contribution to your results and your company's bottom line. When we conducted studies of buyers in physician's offices (including doctors, nurses, and office managers), we discovered that customers who simply know their salespeople by name were 90 percent likely to stay loyal. We also found that the greater the degree of "live" interaction between salespeople and their customers via personal meetings and telephone calls, the higher the customers' satisfaction and loyalty levels, and the higher the percentage of business that customers award their vendors.

Customers want more contact with their salespeople, but salespeople are having a difficult time fulfilling this expectation because they are distracted by a variety of other demands on their time. The result is the fifth customer rule predicting world-class sales success: *"You must be easily accessible."*

The Salesperson as a Traveler

Salespeople have always been the "go-betweens" of the business world. They create and maintain the connections between their companies and their customers. They are both metaphoric and literal travelers, moving continuously between sellers and buyers and facilitating the exchange of value. As Craig Wilson, director of corporate marketing at International Paper, told us, "It's about the salesperson bringing the organization to the client, and having the salesperson bring the client to the organization."

Of course, the means by which salespeople "travel" vary widely and are dependent on their sales environments. Some never actually leave their company premises, but are nevertheless traveling to customers via telephone or the Internet. Others travel locally, visiting customers in a relatively small geographic territory. Still others are true globetrotters who are traveling to wherever in the world their customers do business. No matter how far salespeople travel physically, if they wish to earn world-class status, they must fulfill the customer demand for accessibility.

Top-ranked sales forces go to great lengths to meet their customers' accessibility expectations. "When they want you, you have to be there," explained Tom Wolven, regional president at Alling & Cory. "We carry beepers, use car phones, use voice mail. We do everything we can so that even if customers call in the middle of the night—the printers run 24 hours a day—they can still get us. We're their total resource in terms of responsiveness. We even equip our trucks with two-way radios, so if a guy needs his delivery because he's running out of paper, we can divert trucks. We do the whole bit. . . . With this kind of fast-paced sales, you have to be accessible, you have to be responsive, and you have to solve problems—and staying in constant touch is key."[64]

There are two important points in Wolven's statement to emphasize:

Point #1: Technology Is an Enabler of World-Class Accessibility

The best salespeople utilize technology to ensure that the communication channels to their customers are always open. The nine-to-five business day simply does not apply in most industries or in a global economy that spans every time zone. That is why, when we benchmark world-class sales forces, we find that, like Alling & Cory, they are equipped with as many different technologies as they need to maintain customer contact.

There are several codicils worth considering with regard to technological solutions. For instance, when business customers describe salespeople who satisfy their demand for accessibility, they almost never dwell on the communication technologies that the salesperson uses to maintain contact. In other words, the means of communication are of little interest to customers. Beepers, mobile e-mail, instant messaging, and 800 numbers are all well and good, but if salespeople do not actually respond when customers call, they are merely avenues of frustration, no matter how "cutting edge" they are technologically.

Further, experts are beginning to discover that the same technologies that enable sellers to offer their customers 24/7 access wherever they are in world can also stifle the quality of the responses that customers receive. For instance, Swarthmore College professor Kenneth Gergen writes about what he calls the "challenge of absent presence" and how it can negatively impact the effectiveness of face-to-face communication. Absent presence is the odd but increasingly common state in which a person "is physically present, but is absorbed by a technologically mediated world of elsewhere."[65] Picture eating a meal with someone who answers a cell phone and begins an animated conversation with the caller while you are completely ignored just across the table.

In a related idea, former Microsoft VP of corporate and industry initiatives Linda Stone talks about how people are developing a mindset of "continuous partial attention" in order to be able to scan the constant stream of information from their cell phones, mobile devices (such as BlackBerry and Treo), pagers, laptops, and so on, while remaining engaged in their primary activities. Stone does not think that continuous partial attention is a problem in and of itself. However, it can become a problem when it distracts people from their priorities and interferes with the quality of their decisions and interactions with others. "We're not ever in a place where we can make a commitment to anything," Stone recently explained to *Newsweek*. "Constantly being accessible makes you *in*accessible."[66]

The salient point here is that technology does play an important supporting role in satisfying the customer demand for access. But, the fact that it is in place does not fulfill the fifth customer rule in and of itself. Rather, it is *quality neutral*. It enables communication and accessibility. Sometimes, however, the same technologies that enable your customers to contact you can also create barriers to your response effectiveness.

Point #2: The Level and Quality of Response Is the Key to World-Class Accessibility

It is how consistently and how well *you* respond to customers, more than the technology that connects you to them, that is the primary determinant of accessibility in their eyes. This might include your response to a prospect's initial contact with your company, a question or a desired change that arises in the middle of a sales engagement, or an existing customer's call for information or help. No matter when in the customer relationship the call comes, your response is a primary determinant of the outcome.

Responsiveness has been identified as a key characteristic in the customer's perception of service in numerous studies. In 1990, in one of the seminal books on service quality, Valarie Zeithaml, A. Parasuraman, and Leonard Berry reported that customers ranked responsiveness as one of the four highest-rated criteria in service quality. (The other three criteria were reliability, assurance, and empathy.) A year later, Leonard Schlesinger and James Heskett reported in *Harvard Business Review* that a Forum Corporation study had found that more than two-thirds of customer defections were caused by what customers perceived as indifferent or unhelpful responses from sellers. Interestingly, near the peak of the Quality Revolution, both teams reported that tangible product quality was significantly less important to customers than was the quality of the service responses they received from sellers. Compared to the two-thirds of customers defecting over poor response, the Forum study found that only 14 percent of customers defected because of poor product quality.[67]

What qualities actually determine ease of accessibility and a high-quality response in the business customers' eyes? In our studies, we have found that response excellence is defined by and built upon four criteria: how quickly initial contact with the salesperson is established, how soon the salesperson's response is delivered, the ability of the salesperson to respond appropriately, and the quality and follow-through of the response. These criteria—acknowledgment, proximity, preparation, and execution—are the four response protocols of world-class accessibility.

Acknowledgment: The Demand for Confirmation

The first response protocol that world-class salespeople adopt and practice is plain and simple: they quickly and efficiently acknowledge that their customers' messages have been received. This is the most basic response that salespeople can offer their customers. However, the truth is that although customers regularly reach out to sellers, a significant number of them never receive any confirmation that their messages have been received.

Take the lead-generation process as an example. Business-to-business sellers employ marketing departments whose primary responsibility is to generate and collect leads. They spend huge sums of money and energy to entice potential customers to submit Web forms, fill out surveys, mail response cards, and call 800 numbers. Yet, of all of the customers who do take the time to express their interest, many either do not get a timely response, or do not receive any response at all. This is confirmed by a study from the Center for Marketing Communications, which revealed that 72 percent of inquirers are never contacted by a company representative, 43 percent receive requested information too late, and 18 percent never receive the information they request at all.[68]

When salespeople ignore or respond too slowly to leads and other customer messages, they are sending a signal that is invariably interpreted negatively by the prospective customers. The customers are thinking exactly what you would think in their shoes: "If they cannot be bothered with me now, what is it going to be like when I really need to talk to them?" When salespeople do not promptly respond to the inquiries of prospective customers, they miss new business opportunities and potentially profitable relationships.

This situation is exacerbated as the customer relationship progresses. When information is not forthcoming during the sales process, prospects question the wisdom of becoming customers. When existing customers send messages and do not receive confirmation that they have been heard, they turn to competitors. This is particularly true when customers believe that their calls for help are being purposely ignored. Now, they start to see salespeople as evasive, and worse, dishonest. This is when customer defections often become permanent.

Customer problems, even minor ones, demand instant acknowledgment. It is an issue of stress management. Your customers' stress levels rise whenever they experience a problem involving your products and services that they cannot solve themselves. Their stress is a function of two things: insufficient information and insufficient control. That is, they do not have the means to solve their problem, and their access to those means is outside of their span of authority. They must depend on you, their business agent, for help.

Insufficient information and control can be an extraordinarily incendiary combination when it comes to stress. If you are a parent, you probably know exactly how it feels. Picture what happens to the stress levels of new parents when their first child, an infant who cannot communicate discomfort beyond crying, begins running a fever on a Sunday afternoon. The parents have no idea what is wrong or what to do. The baby won't stop crying, and the fever rises. They call their doctor, who, of course, does not answer. The doctor's service promises to send the message, but beyond that cannot provide any help. And then what? The parents sit and wait. The baby screams. The fever rises another degree. They do not know when the doctor's call will come. Is the doctor in town at all? Just starting eighteen holes of golf and three hours away from a reply? The parents' stress levels hit the ceiling.

Now think about what business customers experience when they call sellers for help with their problems. Typically, their calls are routed into a voice-mail system, which, just as typically, will give them no relief. They do not get the knowledge or the control for which they are searching. They are stuck in limbo, experiencing the same kind of stress as the new parent with a sick baby (perhaps not in the same degree, but that depends on the severity of the problem). Worse, their inability to obtain acknowledgment causes the problem and the anxiety to escalate. Ask yourself this: how many times a year do your customers experience this kind of stress in their dealings with your company, and how many times will it take before they decide they will not go through it again?

World-class salespeople alleviate a good portion of this relationship-sabotaging stress simply by ensuring that their customers' messages are acknowledged as soon as they arrive. These salespeople are realists—they know that there are many instances in which they will not be able to fully answer a prospect's questions or solve a customer's problem on the initial call. However, they also know that an instantaneous confirmation that the customer's message has been received and will be addressed eases the customer's mind. It is the first step in an effective response process.

Successful salespeople create and maintain open channels of communication. For instance, one way we try to facilitate the acknowledgment and confirmation of customer contacts at the Chally Group is by disabling the voice-mail routing feature of our phone system during working hours. We know how it feels to call vendors and other businesses that channel all of their calls directly into automated systems, and we want to make sure our customer calls are answered "live." Do you answer your phone whenever you can? Do you forward office calls to your cell phone when you are on the move, or do you rely on voice mail to pick up and store calls to be answered at your convenience? Does your e-mail arrive in real time, or do you download it only when you are ready to address it?

Of course, no salesperson can provide an instant personal response at all times. Salespeople work under tremendous time pressures. They must devote time to prospects, to their existing customers, to their own companies, and like everyone else, they have personal lives too. A measure of the time pressures that salespeople feel was evident in a 2004 Aberdeen Group survey, which found that salespeople themselves valued productivity—that is, the ability to use their time more efficiently—more highly than any other concern, including the quantity and quality of leads.[69]

In recognition of their time constraints, the best salespeople also provide their customers with alternative contacts who can

AN AUTOMATED RESPONSE IS BETTER THAN NONE

If you cannot offer your prospects and customers an instantaneous live response, be sure to provide an automated response. Most e-mail software allows you to create automatic acknowledgment messages. Your voice-mail box and greeting messages can also be customized. Use these messages to tell customers exactly when they can expect to hear from you *and* to offer them alternative contact information for reaching you or others within your company who are prepared to assist them immediately. Make sure that you keep your messages updated. A voice-mail message that informs customers that you were out of the office two weeks ago does not inspire very much confidence that they will be hearing from you anytime soon.

be called upon when the salespeople are not available. These backups are put into place so customers receive contact confirmation at all times. What is your backup system for contact acknowledgment? How do you cover the unpredictable and often unpreventable message overloads that occur in your absence?

Proximity: The Demand for Response Speed

Global *is* local in today's multinational, 24/7 business-to-business environment. Customers expect that their vendors will be accessible wherever in the world the company does business. Vendors know that if one seller does not fulfill that demand, there is a competitor somewhere in the world who will. This is why the second response protocol is proximity.

Salespeople have to be near enough to their customers to deliver a timely response. "Near enough" is a requirement that bears examination. If your customer is a key account, that might mean physical co-location. For instance, Procter & Gamble's sales to Wal-Mart account for almost 17 percent of its annual revenue. Accordingly, the Cincinnati, Ohio–based consumer products giant has more than 200 employees deployed in a dedicated business unit located in Bentonville, Arkansas, Wal-Mart's headquarters. P&G is not alone. The *Arkansas Democrat-Gazette* estimates that Wal-Mart has attracted more than 1,200 first-, second-, and third-tier vendors to the Bentonville area.[70]

Co-location is an extreme response to the demand for proximity, and it is probably not a feasible solution for the vast majority of business-to-business customers. Sometimes, the seller's business model precludes it. Often, the customer's sales volume or geographic location makes it impossible. How do you satisfy the customer demand that you be near enough when you cannot locate a satellite office next door or even within your customers' companies?

It helps to understand that, in terms of customer response, proximity has a mental component as well as a physical one. Customers know that salespeople cannot perform superhuman feats. Nevertheless, they want to feel as if their salespeople are travelers who can leap geographic, political, and cultural boundaries to provide service whenever and wherever it is needed. In this sense, proximity is a state of mind, a confidence in the seller that is supported by the salesperson's ability to frame and deliver responses in a timely manner.

Regular Contact Supports a Sense of Proximity

One way that world-class salespeople create this sense of confidence in their customers is through a program of regular, but *not* rote, contact. Jenkins, the fictional salesperson that American Airlines invented, is clearly an expert at "being there." He has created an active presence in his customer's mind. The best salespeople also proactively contact their customers. They share useful news, seek feedback on benefits achievement, and sometimes, simply do what friends do—keep in touch with each other.

Unfortunately, the average salesperson does not exhibit this behavior. Typically, salespeople only call on customers when they hope to sell new products and services or when there are sales contracts to be renewed. In between sales calls, their operative attitude of "no news is good news" leads them to keep as low a profile as possible. This is unacceptable, even though it is understandable in light of the fact that a high percentage of customer calls do tend to be about problems or service-related tasks. Further, as we have mentioned, time is a constant pressure for salespeople.

The reaction of world-class salespeople to these hard realities is diametrically opposed to the standard behavior. They know that they cannot hide from customers' problems and still keep their business. Instead, they seek out feedback and problems and they encourage customers to contact them as soon as the slightest hint of trouble appears. They also carefully prioritize their schedules in order to make time for discretionary customer contact. To a much larger extent than many salespeople realize, accessibility is a function of time management. In its 2005 annual productivity study, Proudfoot Consulting found that 17 percent of salespeople's time was spent unproductively as "non-value-added time." Salespeople themselves do not realize the extent of this lost time; they estimate that they spend 4 percent of their time on non-value-added activities.[71] Is there lost time that you can reclaim in order to boost your customer contact rates?

Make Sure You Can Act Locally Everywhere Your Customers Do Business

The perception of proximity is important, but eventually that perception will be tested and it will have to stand up to reality. When this happens, business customers judge proximity in term of response time. No matter where in the world or what time zone you are responding from, they will look for the kind of response speed that is typical of a local vendor.

This benchmark was very clear in a 1999 study we conducted to identify performance standards in the medical supply industry, the first of its kind. In it, customers in physicians' offices rated the sales capabilities of a wide variety of suppliers ranging from local firms to regional and national medical suppliers. Even though regional and national firms had far greater resources, customers awarded their highest ratings to the salespeople in local firms. One reason for this was the enhanced levels of contact and faster response that are inherent in doing business locally. (By the way, the local firms also had the highest variation in ratings. Those that were less than excellent tended to fall off the chart, according to customers.)

WORLD-CLASS RESPONSE AT MOTION INDUSTRIES

Motion Industries, North America's largest distributor of industrial maintenance, repair, and operations replacement parts, is one of only two companies whose sales forces have been identified as "best-in-class" twice by business customers over the fourteen years we have been conducting our world-class sales studies. The company's emphasis on localized response is one key factor in that ranking.

"Responsiveness is an integral part of our strategy," explained CEO Bill Stevens. "When we look at systems, when we look at branch locations, we want everything we do to answer the question, 'How does this help us improve the way we can serve the user, the customer?' That's why we have the number of locations we have in the places that we have them. We want to be able to respond to customers quickly, whether it's two in the morning or two on a Wednesday afternoon.

"I think a lot of companies promote 24-hour, 7-day service, and now with cell phones and everything, it's easy to answer a phone," Stevens continued, "but to call a manned facility 24 hours a day and get a person who's there on site, who can do whatever needs to be done, I think that separates us from the rest."[72]

How can you respond locally? Obviously, the easiest way is if you are local to your customer and can literally frame and deliver a response personally. If you are not local, the next best option is to provide your response at a speed that matches a local response. In this case, you might have a local resource whom you can call upon to deliver a response. Or, you can expedite the delivery of the information or the product the customer needs from your location. In any case, the third response protocol, which we will explore next, is also a key enabler of response speed.

Preparation: The Need for Ready Answers

Whether you are next door to your customer or on the other side of the world, you cannot respond in an effective, timely manner unless and until you are prepared. Further, a poorly framed response can often be more frustrating and stress-producing to your customers than no response at all. That is why the third customer response protocol is preparation.

There are three components of preparation that are related to customer response. The first is identifying the kinds of requests customers typically make. The second is the task of gathering the information, materials, and resources that you anticipate will be needed to respond to these standard customer requests. The third is the task of framing your response to specific customer messages as they arrive.

Component #1: Preparation Means Anticipating Request Scenarios

Salespeople cannot begin to prepare to respond to customers until they have some idea of what customers might ask of them. Accordingly, the best salespeople use scenario planning in order to identify the specific customer issues that salespeople in their positions are called upon to resolve.

There are several types of issues that salespeople deal with. There are issues that are generic to all sales activities, which include requests for marketing materials that describe the salesperson's company and products and services. There are also requests for customized product information and data, routine service, and of course, problem-solving, a topic we will consider in depth in the next chapter. In addition, there are industry-specific issues that generate customer requests, such as regulatory certifications and quality documentation.

There is one more type of customer issue to consider, too: the wholly unexpected request. These are customer requests for action that come out of the blue, such as unique information needs and problems. Unexpected customer requests have only two things in common: they are inevitable and they cannot be foreseen. This is not to say, however, that efficient, high-quality response is impossible; your preparation for the expected can also enhance your readiness for the unexpected.

Component #2: Preparation Means Access to Resources

Effective response is facilitated by the accessibility of the information and other resources needed to fulfill customers' requests. These resources might be marketing materials, such as product brochures, that have been requested by prospects. They might be case studies, specification sheets, or ROI calculations that support the sale. Or they might be any of the myriad resources that existing customers require when they experience problems or when they turn to their vendors for performance data, service confirmations, or information regarding new solutions. In every case, the speed of response is impacted by the availability of the resource required to fulfill the customer's request.

As the best salespeople consider each of the customer message scenarios they might expect, they create lists of the resources needed to fulfill them. Then, they either arrange to have these resources within their reach or they ascertain where the resources are located and how they can be provided to customers most efficiently. For example, if the resource is product information requested by a prospect, the salesperson will know the address at which it resides on the corporate Web site or will have digital files stored and ready to e-mail, or hard copies ready to seal in an overnight envelope and ship. By having the resources that they need literally or figuratively at hand, they never keep prospective customers waiting so long for information that when it finally arrives, the customer wonders what it is and why it was sent.

Component #3: Preparation Means Offering a Game Plan

Most customers are reasonable. They do not expect that all of their requests, no matter how complex, will be resolved in a single phone call. Too often, however, vendors' responses are enough to strain the patience of even the most reasonable customer. One of the most common and frustrating customer experiences is calling a vendor with a service issue or a request and

---

PREPARING FOR THE UNEXPECTED

Former New York City mayor Rudy Giuliani identifies "relentless preparation" as one of the fundamental principles of effective leadership. He credits Judge Lloyd McMahon, for whom he clerked fresh out of law school, with teaching him the importance of preparation. Years later, on September 11, 2001, Giuliani led New York City through one of the most traumatic examples of the unexpected in U.S. history. Here is what he realized as he responded to an unthinkable situation:

We had plans that were written out. We used to rehearse them. When an emergency happened, we would go back and change our plan to reflect things we thought we could do better. But, we didn't have a plan for airplanes being used as missiles. All of a sudden, the words of Judge McMahon came back into my head: If you prepare for everything, you will be prepared for the unanticipated and it will just be a variation. And that is what this was. Every decision that I was making and passing on was coming out of a game plan. I realized this is a high-rise fire, this is a building collapse, this is an airplane crash, this is a terrorist attack. We have plans for all of those things. So, all I was doing was borrowing from those plans. The point: if you prepare for everything you can anticipate, you will be prepared for the unanticipated.[73]

---

being handed off to one unprepared employee after another. To add insult to injury, this handoff process usually requires that the customer must retell her entire story at each stop. Customers may not expect instant execution, but they do expect their calls to generate constructive, efficient action.

World-class salespeople meet this expectation by being prepared to take over the management of the customer's request and communicate an action plan on the first response. They know that a ready answer must also be an informed answer. Whenever possible, they have a plan in place to respond to the customer. If they are returning a call, they are ready to confirm the customer's request and address the need. (Sometimes, if they have enough information regarding the customer's request and it is relatively simple, they are calling to confirm that the required action has already been executed.) When they are receiving the customer's call directly or responding with information, they have a series of action plans at hand from which to choose. For instance, if the customer has a problem, the salesperson will have a series of questions designed to identify probable causes and begin the resolution process. Whatever response is required, the best salespeople are ready to get involved and act as surrogate managers as soon as they accept their customers' calls.

Execution: The Demand for Response Quality and Feedback

Of course, all the acknowledgment, proximity, and preparation in the world cannot overcome the failure to properly execute the fulfillment of customer requests. Execution is the final response protocol, and it encompasses the communication and accessibility expectations that customers have of salespeople during the action phase of response.

We have already seen that successful salespeople personally accept full responsibility for the customer's satisfaction. When things go wrong, they do not blame the company, the shipping department, the technical service group, somebody else's product, or anything or anyone else. They take it upon themselves to follow through with the customer, even when other people are needed to reach a resolution. They communicate regularly and commit to a completion date and level of effectiveness. When served by an effective salesperson, customers no longer see their problems dumped into an abyss, nor do they have to listen to a software person blaming the hardware, or any of a dozen other excuses. It is this mindset that informs world-class response execution.

Ironically, it is possible to perfectly execute a response to a customer and, in the process, still alienate the customer severely enough that the customer will continue to be dissatisfied. For instance, salespeople will often answer customer requests with a well-meant but nebulous statement, such as, "I'll get right on that and call you back." A statement like that might momentarily assuage a customer's stress, but what does it mean? It does not answer critical questions, such as: When will the salesperson return? What is being done? When will the request be fulfilled? Accordingly, the first issue that customers want addressed is the *response plan*. They want to know what the salesperson plans to do, how long it should take, and the resolution that they can expect.

The second issue of execution applies to the many customer situations that require multiple actions or extended periods of time to resolve. In these cases, the customers want to know whether the response is progressing according to plan, what has been discovered along the way, and what, if any, adjustments are being made to the response plan. The best salespeople are very aware of "wait times" involved in their responses to customers. Wait times occur while the customer is waiting to be acknowledged, between the initiation of a response and its completion, and often, between phases of the response. How customers perceive their wait time is a major determinant in how satisfied

The Perception of Wait Time

When keeping customers waiting is unavoidable, an understanding of their psychological perceptions of the wait state can offer insights into how to make those waits *feel* less onerous. During his tenure at Harvard, David Maister, now a leading consultant in the management of professional service firms, articulated these eight "principles of waiting":[74]

- Unoccupied time feels longer than occupied time.
- Preprocess waits feel longer than in-process waits.
- Anxiety makes waits feel longer.
- Uncertain waits are longer than known, finite waits.
- Unexplained waits are longer than explained waits.
- Unfair waits are longer than equitable waits.
- The more valuable the service, the longer the customer will wait.
- Solo waits feel longer than group waits.

they are with the execution of the response. As in the process of acknowledgment, stress is the issue here. If customers are not partners in the response and are not kept informed of progress, they experience higher stress levels. Thus, *progress reports* are an essential element of world-class response.

The third issue of response execution involves *contingency planning and contact alternatives*. As we have seen, the twin realities of customer response are that there are times when sellers cannot execute to commitment, and there are also times when salespeople must be with other prospects and customers. In these cases, the salesperson should have alternatives to offer the customer. These alternatives should include contingency plans that can ensure that salespeople can meet their response commitments. They should also include alternative contacts within the salesperson's organization who are aware of the response plan, can manage it in the salesperson's absence, and most important, can ensure that the communication flow to the customer is not interrupted.

The final issue in response execution is *confirmation and feedback*. When the fulfillment of customer requests is complete, the best salespeople confirm that their customers have received the responses that they expected. These salespeople are also soliciting customer feedback regarding the origins and causes of their requests and the execution of the response. The best salespeople use this information to improve their own accessibility and response protocols. Further, they communicate this information back to their companies, where it can be used to streamline customer processes, improve products and services, and prevent future problems.

The best salespeople are always striving to become more accessible to their customers. Further, they do not presume that being "reachable" is enough to satisfy their customers' expectations of accessibility. Instead, they are reaching *out* to make physical and emotional connections. In addition to loyalty and a larger share of wallet, customers reward salespeople who are accessible in kind. In other words, they provide greater levels of access to their managers and to their internal operations. This enables salespeople to better fulfill each of the other customer rules.

CHAPTER 8

"You Must Solve Our Problems"

O n August 4, 1997, the Teamsters walked off the job at United Parcel Service, Inc. (UPS). A nationwide shipping crisis ensued the moment the company's 185,000 employees stopped work. At the time, they were making 80 percent of the nation's package deliveries. Atlantic Healthcare Products, an established regional supplier of medical and surgical supplies in Westbrook, Maine, faced a dilemma. Ninety-eight percent of its orders were shipped via UPS.

Tom Forst, Atlantic's president, called the strike "a logistics nightmare." The sales force picked up the slack and began hand-delivering customer orders. In fact, Atlantic's salespeople delivered all of the orders throughout the fifteen-day strike. "[A]fterwards," remembered Forst, "customer loyalty to the company was at an all-time high. They truly appreciated the enormous effort put forth by the sales force. We turned a potential disaster into a huge success as far as the customers were concerned." In 2000, Atlantic Healthcare's customers ranked it as the best distributor in the Northeast region in our Physicians' Office World-Class Sales Survey.

We have heard many similar stories in the years we have been investigating best-in-class sales practices. There was the order delivered to a new doctor just opening his first office, which was missing a scale; the sales rep, from Lafayette, Louisiana–based Estorge Surgical Supply Co., drove three hours to deliver a replacement borrowed from another customer. There was the devastating flood that knocked out a hospital's power, causing the destruction of its lab's inventory; a sales rep from Louisville, Kentucky–based Laboratory Supply Co. arranged a replacement delivery for the next day, Easter Sunday. There was the Fort Hood, Texas, Army post, which needed 1,000 doses of hepatitis A vaccine by 7:30 P.M., but neglected to inform the manufacturer until 11:30 that morning. In this case, the catalog seller, Cincinnati, Ohio–based Besse Medical Supply, made sure

---

WHO RUNS WHO?

Do you run your territory, or does it run you? It is an old sales canard, but it is particularly appropriate when it comes to solving customer problems. Unlike the vast majority of salespeople, world-class salespeople *expect* the unexpected problem. They do not know exactly what problems they face, but they do plan ahead in order to be ready to solve problems when they appear. They create response plans to common problems ahead of time and build resolution times into their schedules.

Instead of bouncing between the constant demands of their territories, the best salespeople are able to qualify customers' problems in much the same way that they would qualify a prospect. They seek to prioritize problems by severity, and they offer solution alternatives that include varying response speeds and comprehensiveness of solution. These salespeople realize that every customer problem also contains a personal challenge that belongs to the salesperson alone: "Given all of my responsibilities, how will I be able to resolve this problem to the customer's satisfaction?"

the order got to the airport, was properly handled, and delivered an hour and a half ahead of deadline.[75] The stories differ, but the moral is always the same: customer problems are both the dark cloud and the silver lining of business-to-business sales.

They are the dark cloud because they threaten the customer relationship. A customer with a problem is like a lion with a thorn in its paw. All of its attention is focused on the pain. When customers have a problem, it does not matter how strong a relationship you have or how wonderful a solution you offer. The problem is all that they can see. Customer problems are also like a dark cloud in that they consume the already limited "live" selling time of salespeople. In our behavioral studies of salespeople, we have found that salespeople spend the majority of their time dealing with customer problems. They get called because there is an equipment malfunction or a pricing problem or an unexpected backorder or the wrong item was delivered. In fact, salespeople spend approximately 60 percent of their time resolving product and service issues.

What about the silver lining? The silver lining is the opportunity inherent in the efficient and effective resolution of customer problems. Problems are opportunities to secure the customer's loyalty and with it, a larger share of the customer's wallet. They are opportunities to prove that you and your company are committed to delivering your customer's desired results and added value. When appropriate, they are also opportunities to upsell.

It is for these reasons that the best salespeople become expert at managing the many problems that arise in the quest to attain customer results. In doing so, they fulfill the sixth customer rule predicting world-class sales success: *"You must solve our problems."*

The Salesperson as a Troubleshooter

Problem-solving is a task that is integral to selling. The customer-centric sales processes that dominate today's business-to-business environment are essentially problem-solving processes. The sales-person's role is to identify the prospective customers' problems (or unaddressed opportunities) and offer them viable, compelling solutions. Further, in asking for orders and closing sales, salespeople are constantly addressing problems that keep prospects from buying. A customer objection, for instance, is often described as a problem that must be resolved in order to close a sale.

Problem-solving is also a key skill when working with existing customers. Salespeople are constantly called upon to resolve the varied problems associated with the delivery of solution benefits. This kind of problem-solving is a primary component of customer retention and satisfaction. When Bill Lane, formerly CEO and co-owner of Estorge Surgical Supply Co., was asked to explain what distinguishes the world-class salesperson, he said:

> *The distinguishing factor is always the same: the world-class sales rep is the rep that customers always call on to solve major problems, simply because he/she, through many years of hard work, has the expertise to be the consummate problem-solver. The rep that writes the majority of the business is the same rep who is always there when called upon for any reason.*[76]

Salespeople who become experts at solving customer problems are stepping out of their traditional, compartmentalized roles as business writers and deal closers. They take on a new, more essential role in the customer's mind—the *troubleshooter.* Troubleshooters are essential to the management of customer results. They overcome the barriers that stand between customers and the goals they hoped to achieve in purchasing a vendor's products and services.

What makes a great troubleshooter? Interestingly, it is not a question of creative genius. First, the degree of creativity needed to solve a problem depends on the problem. The majority of customer problems have happened and been solved before. In other words, salespeople do not have to reinvent the wheel to resolve the problems. Second, creativity itself is less a matter of genius than the execution of a repeatable process. For instance, when Thomas Edison built his famous "invention factory" in Menlo Park, New Jersey, he was actually institutionalizing a rigorous, consistent process of creativity. In the Menlo Park labs, he successfully pursued the solutions to a wide variety of problems, including finding a practical, durable filament for the light bulb.

The ability to become a world-class troubleshooter is not determined by intellectual ability either. Dorit Wenke and Peter Frensch of Humboldt University at Berlin studied the relationship between intellect and problem-solving and concluded: "[T]here exists no convincing evidence that would support a causal relationship between any intellectual ability, on one hand, and complex explicit or implicit problem-solving competence, on the other hand." What factors did enable effective problem-solving, according to the professors? They found that there is "good evidence that differences in complex problem-solving, both explicit and implicit, are tied to differences in task knowledge and strategy."[77]

Our studies of world-class salespeople support this finding. *What you know* and *how you approach the problem-solving process* are more important than raw brainpower and creativity. Before we explore these two practical factors, though, there is a third factor that supports and enables effective problem-solving: your mental attitude.

The Mindset of the Troubleshooter

Your mindset determines how you respond to customer problems. When salespeople are confronted with problems and attempt to hide or shift responsibility or affix blame, they are working from a mindset that defines problems in a purely negative light. In doing so, they miss the opportunities and the rewards inherent in becoming an effective troubleshooter.

World-class salespeople approach customer problems with a fundamentally different mindset. It is a mindset that is driven by four realizations:

Realization #1: Problems Are Inevitable

The reality lurking behind all human endeavors, including business-to-business selling, is that errors and other kinds of problems are commonplace. Even a cursory look at the research on the subject reveals that every vendor makes mistakes—three to five times a year on average in major accounts—and that every buyer experiences problems. Customer problems are not exceptions to the rule; they are the rule.

In accepting the inevitability of customer problems, the best salespeople are neither excusing problems nor dismissing them as routine and acceptable. All problems are serious to customers, and there are few things more infuriating to them than having their problems shrugged off as inconsequential. Rather, in accepting the fact that problems are inevitable, salespeople are acknowledging that problems do occur, and that is the attitude that sets the stage for constructive response.

This realization manifests itself in two ways. First, when salespeople know that problems will occur, they equip themselves to deal with them in advance. They identify common customer problems, prepare the resources needed to resolve them, and keep those resources ready and at hand. Second, when salespeople expect problems, they can also prepare their customers. If customers know that certain problems can occur, they are not blind-sided if and when they do. They understand what is happening and they know that their salespeople are prepared to help them. Thus, the stress of the unknown is eliminated and the stress of not being in control is reduced—both for salespeople and for their customers.

How Stress Impacts Problem-Solving

"Problem-solving is a stressful activity," writes Dr. Victor Newman, formerly chief learning officer at European Pfizer Research University. He finds that in our natural desire to avoid stress, we tend to fall into four traps that negatively impact our ability to effectively address and solve problems:

- **Stereotyping,** in which we only see what we want or expect to see
- **Repertoire,** in which we become stuck in an established, but often limited, selection of preferred solutions
- **Visibility,** in which we become unable to see a problem until we find someone else who has seen it and solved it before us
- **Restricted perspective,** in which we reduce the true dimension of the problem until we mistake the next, emergent activity as the whole problem[78]

Realization #2: Problem-Solving Is a Positive Challenge and a Valuable Opportunity

Salespeople often perceive customer problems in a negative light. All that they see is the lost time, the cost, and the damage to customer relationships that problems can cause. Customers are very sensitive to the behavioral cues that these negative perceptions produce in salespeople. Right or wrong, customers often interpret these cues as an unwillingness on the part of the salespeople to accept responsibility for the problem or to help resolve it. This exacerbates the already negative stereotypes of salespeople that lurk in the dark corners of customers' minds, and it increases the stress that problems naturally cause. Customers then react defensively and the result becomes a self-fulfilling prophecy. Salespeople expect customer problems to result in negative outcomes and, lo and behold, they do.

World-class salespeople also create self-fulfilling prophecies around customer problems. The difference is that their prophecy is a vision of successful problem resolution and a strengthened customer relationship. Thus, they enter customer problems with a positive frame of mind.

These salespeople remain focused and confident while looking for solutions. In fact, we have found that they are generally optimistic that they can work through any customer issue and provide a satisfactory outcome. They see problems as professional challenges and address them with energy and assurance. Even better, their attitudes are infectious. Customers quickly come to understand that their problems are going to be among the one in seven that Gallup polls have discovered are "handled at excellence."[79] Again, customer stress is reduced and the odds of a positive outcome are enhanced.

Realization #3: Blame Is Counterproductive

Blame is the nemesis of productive problem-solving. Yet, far too often, salespeople approach customer problems by trying to establish who is to blame. In the process, they alienate their customers, undermine the business relationship, and oftentimes create barriers to problem resolution that cannot be overcome. Worse, some salespeople go so far as to define "customers with problems" as "problem customers." In doing so, they always and automatically shift the blame to the customer with all of the attendant damage that causes to the customer relationship.

Customers usually see the "blame game" as a thinly disguised ruse that vendors use to duck the responsibility for and the cost of problem resolution. Sometimes, unfortunately, they are right. Anyone whose computer malfunctions has probably dealt with the institutionalized finger-pointing that goes on between hardware and software manufacturers. No matter which manufacturer you call, you are told that the problem has been caused by the other. Or perhaps you have attempted to use your purchase in a way that is forbidden and, of course, voids the small print in the warranty. In any case, the blame is affixed and the customer is left with an unresolved problem.

The problem with the blame game is that anytime the finger ends up pointing at the customer or even at another vendor, it becomes a lose/lose game for customers and for salespeople and their companies. This is because business-to-business customers do not care who is to blame. They care only about getting the results that they desired from their purchases. When they do not get those results, no matter who is to blame, the seller is going to be the ultimate loser.

World-class salespeople avoid the issue of blame whenever possible. They realize that they must identify the source of a customer's problem in order to ensure that it is properly resolved and to prevent it from recurring, but they investigate problems using questions and language that avoid the appearance of accusation. Even if it becomes clear that a customer has caused a problem, the best salespeople remain in the role of customer advocate. They do not act as judges; instead, they help the customer understand what needs to be done to avoid the problem in the future without assigning blame.

Most notably, the best salespeople will shoulder the blame and set the tone for successful problem resolution by responding constructively. They know that they are often their customer's most direct link to their companies and that they may well end up bearing the brunt of the customer's frustration. They are willing to act as emotional lightning rods, and they respond to anger with empathy.

Realization #4: The Salesperson Is Personally Accountable for Problem Resolution

Finally, the effective troubleshooter's mindset is one of management and responsibility. When confronted with the specter of customer problems, many salespeople will pass the buck. They refer their customers to service and/or support staff instead of taking direct responsibility for resolving their customers' problems.

This is an unproductive attitude for many reasons. For one, the internal staff at many business-to-business sellers is often neither equipped to effectively resolve customer problems nor particularly customer-centric. For another, there is often no one in

---

ATTITUDE OPENS THE ROAD BACK

Xerox Corporation had been one of Wachovia Corporation's major vendors for twenty years when Wachovia decided to end the relationship. "We really weren't doing a great job in supporting this customer," frankly admitted Xerox CEO Anne Mulcahy, "so, they cancelled the whole Xerox contract."

Mulcahy responded by writing a letter to Wachovia's CEO: "[T]he purpose of the note is to say thank you," she recalled writing. "You have been a great customer and I hope we have had the opportunity to say thanks often, but now particularly that we know we screwed up. You made a different choice. We respect it." And in addition to taking responsibility for the problems that caused Wachovia to switch vendors, she also offered to serve as a troubleshooter: "We are going to help you transition to that choice because you don't want to disrupt your business."

As it turned out, Wachovia's CEO and his team had been working out how to respond when they lost customers. He circulated Mulcahy's note and invited her to meet with his team. "You know," Mulcahy recalled three years later, "we are starting to do business with this customer and I don't think we would have been there unless we had taken the opportunity to thank them for the relationship over time and acknowledge that we screwed up. . . . Instead of packing our bags and pulling out of town, we are going to have to learn how to stay committed to really learning from it and earning the business back."[80]

---

the seller's company who understands the customer, and thus the environment in which the problem has occurred, as well as the salesperson does. Further, the customer will now believe, with some basis in fact, that the salesperson simply cannot be bothered to provide any service that is not directly related to getting a new sale. For all of these reasons, the odds of successfully resolving the problem become more remote, and it becomes ever more likely that the problem, even if it is successfully resolved, will cause a breach in the salesperson's relationship with the customer.

This final realization in the troubleshooter's mindset is actually a direct extension of the first customer rule. First and foremost, world-class salespeople are focused on customer results. Because problems interfere with the achievement of those results, the best salespeople, as surrogate managers, are accountable for addressing and resolving those problems. They take personal responsibility for the problem-solving process and they remain engaged until a solution is reached.

In fact, we find that the best salespeople do not wait for their customers to discover problems. If a problem is emerging or a solution is not delivering the results it should, they will point out the problem to the customers themselves and offer alternatives for resolution. They are proactive troubleshooters in the sense that they will seek out problems without prodding from their customers. They also regularly and actively probe their customers for problems. They ask for feedback and suggestions for improvement on a continuous basis. This practice not only prevents small frustrations from escalating into more serious and severe problems; as we will see in Chapter 9, it also uncovers new opportunities for expanding the customer relationship.

The Mechanics of Problem-Solving

Solving customer problems is always a process of managing the unexpected. The challenge that salespeople face whenever customers call them with problems is to draw on all of their resources, experience, and contacts in order to piece together the most effective and timely solutions they can muster. The best way to consistently meet this challenge is to impose some order on the problem-solving process. Your problem-solving strategy, or how you go about solving problems, as we mentioned earlier, is one of the primary factors that determine problem-solving success.

Twenty years ago, Penn State University School of Public Affairs professor James Ziegenfuss Jr. studied a variety of industries to learn how organizational troubleshooters resolved complaints from customers, patients, and employees, too. He discovered that while individual methods varied, "there seem to be five steps that are central to this process."[81] In problem-solving terms, these are:

- Identify the problem
- Investigate the problem
- Report the investigation results
- Develop the response to the problem
- Manage the response plan to ensure resolution

In the case of simple problems, Ziegenfuss found that these steps often melded together and occurred very quickly. For instance, in an automated environment, a customer may call a salesperson about a billing error and the salesperson may be able to locate the invoice, investigate and confirm the error, and issue a credit in a single phone call. In more complex problems, however, the process may stretch out over days or weeks or more. For instance, a problem caused by an intermittent failure in a process control system may require extended periods of remote diagnosis or the dispatch of a programmer to the customer's plant. But, whether the problem is simple or complex, moving through a process similar to these five steps will expedite resolution.

Step #1: Identify the Problem

When customers call salespeople with problems, the first thing that they are seeking is an advocate. Sometimes, they know what is wrong. Other times, they know that they are not getting the results that they desired, but they don't know why. Sometimes, they are coherent and dispassionate. Other times, they are frustrated and angry. But, no matter what they know and how they feel, they are looking for a sympathetic hearing.

Listening is what the best salespeople do at this stage of problem-solving. They do not refer their customers elsewhere, even if they can determine that the problem will have to be addressed by someone else within their company. They do not jump to conclusions, even when they are sure they know what the problem is and how to solve it. Instead, they hear the customer out.

This process of listening serves several purposes. For one, it allows customers to vent their frustrations. No one likes to be on the receiving end of an angry call, but allowing customers to complain, without interruptions or excuses, plays an important role in beginning the journey toward resolution. After the best salespeople have heard their customers out, they take the opportunity to apologize or, if the problem was clearly not one caused by their company, at least empathize with the customer. In doing so, salespeople align themselves with their customers' best interests and reaffirm their intention to serve as advocates.

Listening is not simply an exercise in mollification; it is also the first step in understanding your customers' problems. This is ground zero for analyzing what has happened or is happening to the customer. Salespeople who are effective troubleshooters listen to their customers' descriptions of their problems for the clues that will lead them to the root causes of the trouble.

Finally, the best salespeople use the first step in problem resolution to confirm that their understanding of their customers' view of the problem is complete and correct. They repeat what they have heard, offer an initial response process based on their preliminary understanding of the problem, and then, when customers agree with that process, they assume management of and accountability for the problem.

Step #2: Investigate the Problem

All customer problems require some kind of investigation. Salespeople must confirm that the problem has actually occurred, and uncover its full dimensions. The more complex the problem and the more people it involves, the more involved this investigation becomes. Typically, the best salespeople are willing to go beyond standard customer service processes and procedures to uncover the cause of the problem.

Root cause is a primary issue in this step of problem-solving. Too often, salespeople mistake the symptoms of problems for their causes. Their customers tell them *what* is happening—that is, they describe a symptom—and instead of taking the time to discover *why* it is happening, the salesperson sets off to cure the symptom. Of course, if the actual cause of a problem is not addressed, the problem will recur, often manifesting new symptoms. Any doctor can tell you that addressing a problem's symptoms does not solve the problem.

Skillful questioning supports the ability to identify root causes. One of the techniques used in Toyota's renowned manufacturing system is a simple investigative technique called "5 Whys." When defects occur, Toyota's employees analyze them in a step-by-step fashion by repeatedly asking "Why?" until they reach the root causes of the problem. Why is the part defective? Because the punch press malfunctions every fifth punch. Why does the press malfunction? Because the punch arm does not fully retract. Why doesn't the punch arm fully retract? Because every fifth part is fed into the press too quickly and triggers the arm before it is in the proper position. Why . . .? and so on.

Observation is a second skill that supports thorough problem investigation. There is no substitute for witnessing a problem firsthand and being able to examine all of the things that are going on around it, that is, seeing it in the context in which it is occurring. The pitfalls of being unable to directly observe a problem are illustrated by the apocryphal stories of hapless computer support reps who spend extended periods on the phone with customers whose PCs are not working only to find out that a cable is not properly connected or a power cord is loose. Whenever appropriate, the best salespeople will go to the source of the problem to see what is happening for themselves. As Yogi Berra suggested, "You can observe a lot by watching."

Finally, the best salespeople fully investigate problems by speaking with everyone involved. They know that problems can appear to have different causes and different implications when seen from different positions. They strive to see all sides of the customer's problem and to understand it from as many perspectives as they can before attempting to design solutions to resolve it. To accomplish this, they speak with employees within their customer's companies as well as employees in their own companies.

Step #3: Report on the Problem

Once salespeople complete their problem investigations, but before they can formulate resolutions, they must report their findings *and* gather feedback and input from both their own companies and their customers. If the problem is to be resolved successfully, both parties will have to support the salesperson's findings and whatever solution he or she proposes.

Reporting the results of problem investigations internally is an important step in the resolution process. Your company needs to ascertain its own role in the problem. Further, you need some guidelines regarding the type and level of responses your company deems appropriate to solve the problem.

There is another very good reason to report your findings about customer problems to your company as quickly as possible: the costs that sellers incur when they respond slowly and/ or poorly to customer problems can often be enormous. AMR

Research calculated that in 2005 almost as many cars were recalled as were sold. It found that detection-to-correction time for defects in the auto industry averaged 120 days, and ranged as high as 220 days. The cost of these defects, including service, labor, parts, and brand impact, ran up to $1 million *per day*.[82] Clearly, any information that salespeople can provide to their companies that will help prevent problems and/or more quickly and effectively address existing problems is highly valuable.

Customers, too, need a full accounting of the causes of their problems. As the customer's surrogate manager, it is the salesperson's responsibility to offer an honest report. If the seller is the cause of the problem, an admission of responsibility goes a long way toward defusing customer frustration. If the problem's causes are internal to the customer, a tactful recounting, without assigning blame, sets the stage for successful resolution.

The best salespeople also use this opportunity to elicit feedback from the customer. They find out what the problem has cost the customer and what the customer expects in terms of a resolution. This feedback serves to inform the next step in the problem-solving process and helps the salesperson frame a response that best serves the customer.

Step #4: Develop Problem Resolutions

As we mentioned earlier, success in problem-solving depends less on creative genius than it does on "task knowledge." For salespeople who are facing customer problems, this task knowledge is based upon their understanding of their customer's businesses and the ways in which their customers use their products and services. Their task knowledge also includes their understanding of the actions and processes within their own companies that may be contributing to the customer's problem.

Just as the best salespeople use their knowledge of the customer's business and operations to create tailored solutions, they also use this knowledge to create tailored problem resolutions.

PROBLEM-SOLVING AUTHORITY IS ESSENTIAL

One of the most common barriers we find to effective problem-solving is the limited authority of salespeople. When salespeople are not empowered to make decisions or must delay their responses for managerial approval, their value and competence are undercut in the customer's eyes. Typically, what happens in these instances is that the customer perceives the salesperson as ineffective and goes directly to whoever has the authority to make the decision. Afterward, they are often reluctant to work directly with the salesperson again, preferring to deal directly with the real decision-maker.

The best sales organizations give their salespeople the authority they need to personally resolve a range of issues without waiting for a manager's approval. When sellers do not grant this authority, we find that the best salespeople tend to assume it for themselves, working through back channels and their own networks to quickly and effectively resolve their customers' problems.

They know that companies are living systems, and that in living systems, *biovariability* is an important consideration in any intervention. It is the biovariability among people that causes their bodies to respond differently to the same medications or diet or exercise. The effectiveness of customer problem resolutions is subject to corporate biovariability—because individual companies respond differently, what works for one customer may very well not work for another. In recognition of this fact, the best salespeople avoid one-size-fits-all resolutions or use them only after confirming that they will work appropriately for the customer with whom they are currently engaged.

In tailoring resolutions, world-class salespeople always stay focused on the customer's results. Too often, sellers act as if replacing a defective part or offering a credit is enough to ensure the customer' satisfaction and loyalty. But if the customer's operations have been halted, or a relationship with one of its own customers has been damaged, the stakes become exponentially higher. In fact, in business-to-business sales, problems cannot be considered fully resolved until their impact on the customer's results has been rectified. When the best salespeople formulate solutions, they start with the customer's desired end state and work backward from there.

As we talk to business customers, they tell us that the best salespeople are capable of solving problems in nontraditional ways. In other words, these salespeople think outside the box in terms of their responsibilities to the customer *and* the kinds of resolutions they will offer. They do so by recasting their knowledge and resources to solve customer problems in new and highly effective ways. The classic example of problem-solving is one in which a salesperson formulates a solution to a problem that is clearly outside his or her area of responsibility. Consider the paper salesman, for instance, who on discovering that his customer's press has jammed during a job with a tight deadline, arranges to have the job printed at another shop and delivered back to the customer in time to meet the deadline. These kinds of solutions require that problems be reformulated and that the salesperson's resources and knowledge be applied in new ways. That is the not-so-mysterious basis of the kind of creativity in problem-solving that results in exceptionally high levels of customer satisfaction and loyalty.

Step #5: Manage the Resolution of the Problem

Many failures in resolving customer problems can be traced back to the salesperson's unwillingness or inability to shepherd a solution through to its proper conclusion. Execution is especially critical with regard to customer problems because their resolution often requires actions that must occur outside the everyday tasks and responsibilities of the people involved. If no one has the formal responsibility for managing the resolution, it will often get hung up as it travels outside the established channels. A credit may sit on a supervisor's desk awaiting approval, or a phoned-in request for a replacement part will get waylaid in the rush of everyday business. When these kinds of things happen, the problem becomes compounded. Customers become doubly frustrated with problems that either will not go away or spawn a host of new problems. Worse, they now also feel as if no one in the seller's organization cares.

This is why the last step in problem-solving, but surely not the least, is the execution of the resolution. The best salespeople assume management of customers' problems, which includes remaining engaged until customers confirm that the problem has been resolved and they are satisfied. This may involve working with internal people, or finding external resources to provide the solution. In either case, the salesperson retains personal accountability for the final results. No matter how simple or complex the problem, however, it remains incumbent on the salesperson to supervise the progress of the problem's resolution and report back to the customer.

The best salespeople also provide feedback on the effectiveness of their problem resolutions to their own companies. They share ideas for the successful resolution of customer problems with their colleagues and in doing so, help their companies boost their organizational capabilities as problem-solvers.

In their willingness to take accountability for resolving their customers' problems, world-class salespeople demonstrate and reinforce their commitment to customer results and long-term relationships. Their open and positive response to problems encourages customers to see these salespeople as valuable business partners and to share ever-increasing amounts of information about the challenges that they face. This sets the stage for the successful fulfillment of the next and last customer rule.

CHAPTER 9

"You Must Be Innovative in Responding to Our Needs"

Like e-commerce before it, the rise of outsourcing, which is the ultimate expression of managing the customers' results, has been a dominant and continuing business theme in recent years. In the first quarter of 2006, the total value of large outsourcing contracts (those worth $50 million and more) was $22.6 billion—a rise of 173 percent over the first quarter of 2005.[83] But for all of the demand for and growth in outsourcing, there is also evidence of a disturbing undertow running beneath the growing market that should have the sellers of these services paying careful attention.

It turns out that enough business customers are canceling their contracts and reasserting control over their outsourced operations that a word has been coined to describe the process—*insourcing*. The largest of these broken deals make headlines in the business press. In September 2004, just two years after the deal was inked, JPMorgan Chase & Co. canceled a $5 billion, ten-year outsourcing contract with IBM. In May 2005, one year after its deal was signed, Sears prematurely ended a $1.6 billion, ten-year outsourcing pact with Computer Sciences Corporation. In May 2006, Diebold, Inc., announced that it would take a charge against earnings of seven cents per share to cut three years from its seven-year outsourcing deal with Deloitte Consulting.[84]

Given the complexity of outsourcing business services and processes, it is not surprising that some of these partnerships fail. But in 2005, Deloitte itself studied twenty-five companies that were spending a combined total of $50 billion on outsourcing and discovered that 70 percent of the companies had "unsatisfactory outsourcing experiences, encountering two to ten problems." The problems were wide-ranging, but the majority of them fell into two categories: first, customers did not achieve the expected cost savings; second, the improvements that the customers hoped to achieve by applying the vendors' best practices, quality, and innovation to their services or processes never materialized. Deloitte reported that 57 percent of outsourcing customers said they entered into contracts expressly for the service or process improvements, "but 31 percent of these participants stated vendors became complacent once the contracts were in place." One in five of the companies Deloitte studied said that unless pressured, vendors "fail to provide innovative solutions and process improvements once contracts are in place."[85]

We hear so much about the cost advantages of outsourcing and the opportunities that it provides customers to focus on their own core competencies that we tend to forget this side of the coin: customers are also buying the vendor's expertise. When they sign ten-year contracts, they expect that their outsourcing providers will be delivering a world-class service in each year of the contract. However, if the vendor does not continuously improve the service throughout the contract, that expectation cannot be fulfilled. That is why Delphi Group founder and CEO Tom Koulopoulos, a leading thinker in outsourcing, pegs innovation as a major factor in what he calls "smartsourcing." He writes:

A smartsourcing strategy creates a much more intimate relationship between the organization and its service partner.

*Smartsourcing increases innovation throughout the range of pro-
cess from core to noncore, allowing organizations to focus on their
most critical areas of differentiation and customer value, while
also achieving high levels of innovation in noncore operations.*[86]

Outsourcing is not the only business-to-business market in
which customer demand for innovation is running high. The
reality is that business customers are demanding innovation
and continuous improvement in every product and service that
they buy from vendors. What you are really selling, and what
the customer is really buying, is expertise and your ability to
apply it in new ways to improve the customer's results. As Peter
Luongo, former president and CEO of The Berry Company, a
subsidiary of BellSouth that sells Yellow Pages advertising, told
us, "At the end of the day it's not a plan or even a solution. It's
having the people who can continually modify the plan and
build new solutions." This is the impetus behind the seventh
and final customer rule predicting world-class sales success:
"You must be innovative in responding to our needs."

The Salesperson as an Innovation Alchemist

The seventh customer rule provides a solution to one of the most
difficult challenges facing today's business-to-business salespeople: gaining access to the C-level decision-makers within
customer organizations. As their solutions grow more complex
and more expensive, and as their customers' organizations
grow leaner and less hierarchical, salespeople are finding that
the point of purchase is rising. Instead of selling to purchasing agents and operational managers, many salespeople must
now sell to senior executives in business units and corporate
headquarters.

Salespeople who successfully fulfill the seventh rule enjoy
unfettered access to the C-suite because innovation is a primary

concern among the senior executives of their customer companies. When IBM surveyed 765 CEOs, business executives, and public sector leaders for its 2006 Global CEO Study, it found that 65 percent of them expected to make fundamental changes in their businesses within the next two years. These executives pinpointed *innovation*—in business models, operational processes, and the products and services they bring to market—as a leading factor in their ability to manage these changes and grow their companies and brands.

IBM asked the executives to specify the three most significant sources of this innovation. Surprisingly, only 17 percent of the respondents mentioned their own R&D departments, which are the traditional source of innovation. R&D was next to last on the list of the eight most significant sources of innovative ideas, ahead of academia alone. By contrast, the top three choices were the general employee populations of the executives' companies, their business partners, and their customers (which were named 41 percent, 38 percent, and 36 percent of the time, respectively). This finding led IBM CEO Sam Palmisano to conclude that business leaders "believe that external collaboration across their business ecosystems will yield a multitude of innovative ideas."[87]

The fact that almost 38 percent of senior executives already look to their business partners to provide innovative ideas also explains why salespeople who can apply their products and services in innovative ways find the path to the C-suite easier to navigate. These executives have little or no interest in discussing commonplace or low-level operational problems with salespeople, or anyone else for that matter. If they are aware of such problems at all, they simply delegate their management and resolution to someone farther down the corporate ladder. The executives want to talk to salespeople who can tell them about innovative new solutions that can address strategic-level challenges and open new opportunities for growing their companies.

Today's business-to-business salespeople also have a highly valuable innovation role to play within their own companies. If, as IBM's survey suggests, customers are one of the top three sources of innovation ideas, then salespeople, who often represent their company's closest direct contact with customers, should be in the best position to see and transmit these customer-generated ideas back to their own companies. In fact, this has proven to be the case at General Electric Medical Systems [GEMS]. In their book *Confronting Reality*, Larry Bossidy and Ram Charan write:

> *GEMS, which sells high-tech medical equipment to hospitals, was able to tap a huge aftermarket business because of its intimate knowledge of the medical professionals who use its equipment. The sales team spends a lot of time with doctors in the field, talking with and observing them. That close contact allows them to sort through what doctors really care about. Do radiologists care about resolution, time, or something else? Knowing exactly what the doctor is trying to accomplish with the machinery helps GE Medical focus its research efforts and makes new-product introductions far less hit or miss. GEMS's close relationship with doctors also helped it identify a new aspect of the medical industry it could get involved in: information management. This discovery has driven a fundamental change in the business, from selling products to selling packages of products and services, and has opened a large new growth trajectory.[88]*

Further, it appears that salespeople who actually use their interactions with customers to help their own companies innovate are relatively few and far between. Even though IBM's 2006 Global CEO Study found that customers were the third most valuable source of innovative ideas, the surveyed executives identified their own customer-facing sales and service units as sources of innovation less than half as frequently. Thus, the few salespeople who can effectively transmit ideas back to their companies—that is, salespeople who can channel the voice of the customer—will be highly valued by their own senior managers.

When today's best salespeople respond to their customers' evolving and often unspoken needs with continuous improvement and innovation, they are acting like modern-day alchemists. They are transmuting their company's products and services, and their own expertise, into added value and results

---

CA BROADENS ITS SALES EXPERTISE

CA, formerly Computer Associates, is a company in the process of a turnaround after mismanagement and financial improprieties that resulted in the loss of two-thirds of its senior team, as well as jail terms for four of its top execs. A notable element in this turnaround has been the restructuring of the sales force under Gregory Corgan, formerly IBM's executive VP of worldwide sales.

In the past, CA's sales force had been organized on a brand basis, and each was selling its own products with no incentive to learn about the company's other, related products or to offer them to customers. As a result, says Corgan, "We didn't have a history of managing customers as customers. We had a history of rerolling transactions."

Today, 60 percent of the original sales force has turned over. The company has been reorganized into five product divisions, each with its own sales force. CA also has 270 account directors who manage customer relationships; support specialists who are expert in all of the company's products; and a presales technical staff that can analyze and evaluate the customers' IT architecture. Further, this expertise is supported by a new compensation plan, scheduled to be in place in 2008, which is designed to reward salespeople for aligning the company's software with its customers' business goals.[89]

---

for their customers. Salespeople who succeed in this endeavor find that like the most talented medieval alchemists, who enjoyed the patronage of the powerful rulers of their day, they too become trusted and respected advisors—in this case, at the highest levels of their customers' organizations.

The Three Levels of Alchemical Expertise

Innovation expertise is not easily acquired. No matter how innately talented salespeople are, the knowledge that they must bring to bear to help customers achieve results is usually developed over years of selling. This is one reason salespeople identified as masters of the final rule by the business customers we studied are most often sales veterans. Like sports superstars, such as Tiger Woods and Andre Agassi, great salespeople also require training and experience to hone their innovation skills.

It is, however, worth the work. Once salespeople have attained advanced levels of innovation, they also enjoy high levels of customer credibility. This credibility is dependent upon the timeliness and validity of salesperson's innovative input and contribution. They must be proactive in sharing news that may affect their customers and provide information that is relevant to their customers' problem-solving or decision-making processes. They must also be seen as "clear" channels of communication, presenting facts without bias or embellishment. As Phil Bohay, general manager of customer services for business sales and solutions at Canadian telecommunications company SaskTel, told us, "The key word that I like to use is 'currency' and having 'currency' with the customer. If you haven't got the sort of business acumen and the political acumen to be able to work with your customers and bring real added value in your exchange of ideas and opportunities you can suggest, then you are no longer relevant."

There are three levels of knowledge currency required to build your credibility and to provide your customers with relevant innovative responses and solutions. They are technical expertise, industry expertise, and cross-functional expertise.

Technical Expertise

The first and most basic level of knowledge that supports innovative responses is technical or product-based expertise. This is also the expertise that customers most commonly expect from their vendors. For instance, it is "technology expertise," not cost, that is the most frequently mentioned selection criterion among buyers of outsourced IT services.[90]

Technical expertise has good, better, and best components. Good salespeople become expert in the capabilities of the products and services they are directly responsible for selling. Better salespeople expand their expertise to include not just the products and services that they are charged with selling, but *all* of the products and services their companies offer their customers. The best salespeople take their expertise a step further and become subject-matter experts.

As subject-matter experts, the best salespeople develop and maintain a comprehensive knowledge base of all of the related products and/or services that are available to their customers. They acquire knowledge about competitors' offerings through published information, and supplement it with personal and industry contacts. They stay abreast of the product and service developments in their industry through more formal learning opportunities, such as professional associations, seminars, and trade shows. These salespeople see themselves as continuous learners. They know that change is constant and for expertise to remain relevant, it must be constantly updated.

In assuming the role of subject-matter expert and developing an industry-wide breadth of product and service expertise, the best salespeople become valued resources to their customers. They are recognized for their ability to apply new developments to the customer's workplace. They also always keep their customers' best interests in mind by willingly sharing information, even at the risk of leading the customer to a competitor.

Industry Expertise

The second level of knowledge that the best salespeople apply to customer needs is their expertise in the customer's industry. Salespeople, who are usually calling on a number of business customers in a given industry, see their customers' industries from a far different perspective than individual customers typically see them. From this viewpoint, and fully within the bounds of professional ethics, they can help their customers create a more comprehensive portrait of their markets and competitive environments.

THE ETHICS OF KNOWLEDGE SHARING

The ability to craft innovative responses to customer needs is dependent on knowledge sharing. However, sharing knowledge has limits that must be respected. For instance, if salespeople reveal sensitive customer information in this process, they are breaching their ethical, and perhaps legal, responsibilities. Further, they are harming their chances for creating an open, trusting relationship with the customer who is receiving the information. Customers are naturally reluctant to share information with salespeople who they know do not respect the dictates of confidentiality.

The best salespeople balance the value of sharing their knowledge with the customer demand and desire for confidentiality. They are always aware of sensitivity of proprietary information and never reveal competitive knowledge. When they are in doubt, they gain permission before revealing information. In doing so, they enhance customer trust and access.

World-class salespeople are highly aware of the market trends, including environmental and competitive forces, that are at work within the customers' industries. They take pride in maintaining an in-depth awareness of market issues and strive to be seen as a source of market advice and information to their customers.

Further, the industry knowledge that salespeople can offer their customers is first-person and multidimensional. Salespeople often have a front-row seat as market and product trends emerge in their customers' industries. They know which of their products and services are experiencing high demand, and they see how they are being applied. They use this knowledge to help their customers identify and tap into emerging opportunities.

Cross-Functional Expertise

Most innovations come from the application of existing knowledge in a new context. In 1948, George de Mestral returned from a walk with his dog, and, while removing the burrs attached to his pant leg, was struck by their gripping power. On examining one under a microscope, he realized that its design could be reproduced and used as a fastener. Velcro was born. In the early 1970s, Art Fry, a new-product developer at 3M, used a weak adhesive created by mistake by 3M scientist Spence Silver to make bookmarks for his church hymnal. The Post-it Note was invented.

For salespeople, the ability to apply existing knowledge in new contexts is usually built on their functional expertise. In other words, the best salespeople see how to apply knowledge they gain from one functional area of a business to another. Their cross-functional expertise enables them to apply a variety of different perspectives to generate innovative ways of serving their current customers.

This final level of expertise is the most difficult for salespeople to attain. Professional salespeople, after all, tend to stay in sales. They never receive the benefit of the rotation through a variety of functions that companies offer promising professional managers and fast-track executive candidates. So, unlike managers, whose business knowledge tends to be eclectic, salespeople are usually expert in a single silo—the sales function—which, unless they are selling sales-related products and services, is of little or no use to their customers.

One way that salespeople overcome this barrier and do gain functional experience is by selling products and services in different customer environments. In learning how their company's products and services are used in different industries and in a variety of functional areas within customer companies, salespeople expand their ability to identify and offer innovative ideas. Their frame of reference expands outside the functional silo of sales, and they raise their expertise from the tactical level to a higher level—the so-called 30,000-foot view of the senior executive and the strategic consultant.

At this level, the best salespeople begin to see their customers' companies in new ways. For instance, they come to see a rental car company that buys their goods and services as more than a maintainer and manager of fleets of cars. It becomes a transportation company that is interested in anything that can help it move its customers from one place to another more efficiently. Or a higher level yet, the transportation company becomes a personal services company that is interested in an even broader range of travel-related products and services, such as CRM databases, systems for managing the delivery of cars to customers instead of vice versa, GPS mapping systems, and satellite radios. As the salesperson's perspective expands, so does his or her ability to uncover and fill a host of new opportunities.

The Five Attributes of Innovative Salespeople

It is important to recognize the difference between problem-solving (as we discussed it in the last chapter) and innovation.

Problem-solving is reactive and mainly tactical in nature. The salesperson is responding to a specific problem as defined by the customer—something that has gone wrong somewhere in the delivery of the expected benefits. Innovation, on the other hand, is proactive and more likely to be strategic in nature. The salesperson is often responding to a problem or an opportunity that the customer has not yet recognized and/or clearly defined.

Innovative responses are usually unique combinations of vendor solutions and customer circumstances. Therefore, they are not easily scripted. Although there are formal innovation processes, such as those followed by R&D departments, we find that innovation in sales is more opportunistic in nature. Thus, the best salespeople are able to respond innovatively to customers through application of their own behaviors and skills rather than through the execution of a fixed process. In our studies of world-class salespeople, we have been able to define five of these attributes.

Attribute #1: The Ability to Judge the Innovation Receptivity and Profit Potential of Customers

World-class salespeople know where and when to offer their expertise. These salespeople judge which of their contacts within a customer organization are open to innovation and which are not. Further, they understand that only a certain percentage of their customers will be interested in innovative responses *and* that innovative responses may not be appropriate based on the level of return their own company will reap from a particular customer.

When we studied physicians' office customers within the medical supply industry, we found that customers' receptivity to innovation varied by position. Doctors placed a high value on the salesperson's ability to provide innovative new products and ideas. In fact, this was the attribute in salespeople that they rated as most important. Nurses and business managers, however, were less interested in innovative responses and more interested in the day-to-day concerns of their jobs and the efficient running of their offices. If you translate this finding to the corporate environment, it suggests that your contacts at the highest levels of customer organizations will be more interested in innovative thinking than will your contacts at lower levels of the organizations.

Salespeople must also weigh the receptivity of customers in a larger sense. They have to distinguish between occasional or transaction-based customers and long-term customers who see them in a more strategic sense as business partners. The customer who sees your product as a commodity, who is solely interested in price, and who restricts your access to the purchasing staff is unlikely to be interested in considering your ideas for expanding the company's business into a new market. On the other hand, a customer company that is always asking you to add value to your offerings and that shares its business plans with you is likely to be highly interested in innovation.

Finally, the best salespeople always judge the economic potential of their customer relationships. They choose where to apply their innovation expertise based on this economic potential. They identify and focus their efforts on customers who will provide returns commensurate with the level of innovation expertise that they receive.

Attribute #2: A Commitment to Keep Customers Up-to-Date

Unapplied knowledge has little value in the business-to-business world. So, as the best salespeople continuously gather knowledge, they also actively disseminate it among their customers. They are committed to sharing all three levels of their expertise with customers.

This is not to say that customers are dependent solely on salespeople for information, and certainly, there is no percentage in treating customers as anything other than experts in their own industries and businesses. The best salespeople, however, play a valuable role in keeping customers up-to-date regarding competitors, market trends, regulations, and so on. Given the information glut that many executives are struggling to manage, these salespeople can help customers winnow out the most useful knowledge. They also can serve as sounding boards for their customers.

Perhaps most important, when salespeople focus on knowledge sharing, they begin to craft customer conversations that rise above the monotonous drone of the standard sales pitch. They use the knowledge they have gathered as the basis for open and informative conversations that are focused on the challenges and opportunities the customer faces. When they share what they have learned about the customer's world and the applications that can address the customer's issues, they demonstrate their ability to add value to the customer's business. When they share a finding or an idea that the customer has not heard before, they transform themselves into innovation alchemists.

Attribute #3: A Constant Search for New Applications

The best salespeople are always looking for new ways in which their expertise, products, and services can be applied to their customers' businesses. They understand that products and services do not sell themselves, and they search out creative ways to match their products and services to the diverse needs of their customers. In other words, they continually try to expand their application repertoire.

Hewlett-Packard vice president and "creatologist" Joseph Batista, who began his career in sales at Digital Equipment Corporation (DEC), is a devoted practitioner in this area. After DEC merged with Compaq, Batista created iVelocity, a brainstorming workshop designed to help customers build speed and scale into new business projects by providing them with access to Compaq's product knowledge and implementation experience. "I try to help customer companies accelerate their business plans," explained Batista. "We are so big and have so many hidden assets that neither the customer nor the average sales professional in the field realizes what we can do for them. We try to think about our resources in a different light. We look at what we have, listen to the customer and begin to play out certain scenarios."[91]

As Batista well knows, the constant search for new applications helps salespeople expand their business with existing accounts by utilizing innovative means to answer their needs. It also helps win new customers, particularly among emerging companies, which are usually very appreciative of the knowledge and resources an established business partner can offer them.

Attribute #4: The Ability to Recognize Unspoken Customer Needs

World-class salespeople are constantly searching for the right opportunity to apply their innovation skills. In fact, they are able to identify opportunities that the average salesperson overlooks and answer customer needs that customers themselves often do not recognize.

This is an attribute that Dow Corning has been working hard to inculcate within its sales force. By 2000, Dow Corning's customers were increasingly treating its silicon-based products as premium-priced commodities, and as a result, the company was experiencing lackluster sales and stagnant growth rates. One way it addressed this problem was to segment its customers by their needs. Its price-sensitive commodity customers were given a low-cost product line that they could order via the Internet. In this way, the sales force was able to dedicate its efforts to customers who wanted added value.

Dow Corning trained its salespeople to identify opportunities for innovative responses within their customers' businesses. This resulted in the company offering a variety of new services to support its customers, including translating customer labels into foreign languages, supply chain optimization, and advice on foreign regulatory issues. In one example, Ragnar Avery, a twenty-two-year sales veteran, met with the senior leadership of a customer company, as well as its purchasing and technical staff, and discovered that the customer wanted to reduce its inventory costs. "We were able to provide contract packaging to them in customized form," explained Avery to *CRM* magazine, "and that freed them up to not having inventory anymore—we would, basically, handle inventory. We took a transactional process out of their hands, saving them money and getting us better profitability as well."[92]

Attribute #5: A Willingness to Try the Untested

Finally, the best salespeople are action-oriented when it comes to innovation. They choose their innovation opportunities carefully, but when they identify a viable opportunity to innovate, they respond quickly and without fear.

In studying world-class salespeople, we have found that they are willing to try untested ideas and solutions. They tend not to feel constrained by standard procedures or methods. They value what has proven successful in the past, but are willing to stretch to meet customer requirements, even when this adds extra pressure to their workload or introduces additional risk to the sale.

This attitude often proves to be infectious. These salespeople excite and motivate their customers to explore new areas and experiment with new ideas. This sense of enthusiasm introduces urgency into a sale and encourages action on the customer's part, thus helping to shorten sales cycles and stimulate buying decisions.

Because innovation is by its very nature unpredictable, the best salespeople are also flexible and adaptable in their pursuit and execution of innovative solutions. As they formulate and present innovative responses, they are prepared to change them based on the customer's reactions and input. In addition, as they execute innovative responses, they use their problem-solving skills to resolve unexpected barriers to the successful delivery of results.

In developing the ability to deliver innovative ideas and applications to their customers on a continual basis, salespeople fulfill the final customer rule and cement their ability to win new business and expand existing customer relationships. In completing our examination of the final customer rule, we have also finished answering the second question that we posed in the book's introduction: *What capabilities define the highly effective sales professional?* Now, in the next and final section of the book, we will take a step back and explore the insights that our surveys of business customers have revealed about the composition of the world-class sales organization.

PART FOUR

Eight Questions for Identifying World-Class Sales Organizations

Thus far, we have focused on an in-depth exploration of the customer-defined competencies of the world-class salesperson. We have examined the skills that individual salespeople can and should develop and cultivate in order to fulfill their customers' rules of engagement as well as win an ever-larger share of their wallets. Our primary goal has been to apply the results of our research to help you become a world-class salesperson in your customers' eyes. Now we would like to turn your attention to one final subject: the customer-defined characteristics of a world-class sales organization.

Over the past fourteen years, our research has revealed a great deal about the expectations that business customers have of sales organizations. Prior to this book, we at Chally placed a special emphasis on these organizational lessons. With the support of a distinguished group of sponsors, we identified the characteristics of world-class sales organizations that business customers support with their buying behaviors. With the cooperation of companies that customers awarded best-in-class status, we conducted benchmarking studies to identify their best practices. We published reports and white papers that described our findings. We also communicated the lessons we learned from the world-class sellers and their customers at conferences and seminars around the world. Now, in this final section of the book, we offer them to you in the form of eight questions (illustrated with examples drawn from benchmarking studies of five of the world-class sales award winners and other successful business-to-business sellers) that you can use to identify world-class sales organizations for yourself.[93] The questions are:

- *What drives the company's culture?*
- *How does the company segment its markets?*
- *How efficiently does the company adapt to market changes?*
- *How are customers served by the company's IT initiatives?*
- *How evolved are the company's sales, service, and technical support systems?*
- *How does the company solicit customer feedback and measure customer satisfaction?*
- *How does the company recruit and select salespeople?*
- *How does the company train and develop its sales force?*

If you are a salesperson, these questions can help you determine *where* you can put your knowledge and skills to their best possible use. If you are satisfied with your current position, the answers will help you understand how your company's sales strengths can best support your performance and improve your results. You can use this information to make better use of the resources your company offers. Perhaps you can also practice your "influence without authority" skills and lobby for improvements, if and when they are needed. If you are just beginning your sales career or changing jobs, you can use these eight questions to help you identify an employer who can best support your future success.

If you are a sales executive or manager, the eight questions can help you in many of the same ways. You can use them to assess your current position and future career opportunities. In addition, because you have some managerial power, you can go a step further and identify the strengths and weaknesses of your sales force in order to improve its performance and results. Pay particular attention to those questions that you have the authority to address. They can make an outsized impact on your team's results.

Finally, if you are a senior executive, you can use these eight questions to weigh your company's performance against companies that have fielded the best sales forces in the world. The eight questions will provide you with insights into how to improve the results of your sales force and, more important, how the rest of your company can support and enhance sales results. We hope that you will use our findings to create an entire organization that is capable of achieving sales excellence.

What Drives the Company's Culture?

Corporate culture is the reef of attitudes and behaviors that lies beneath the surface of every business-to-business seller. When this reef is well shaped it can be a protective barrier against competitors. But when it is misshapen, it can sink your company.

Like a reef, a company's culture is a living system. It typically grows and evolves over long periods of time in a process of accretion. Every employee can influence the culture to a small degree, but generally, employees who want to stay with a company must adjust to the culture instead of vice versa. For these reasons, a corporate culture is usually a steady, stable system that is neither quickly nor easily altered. Unfortunately, the market environment in which a company competes will often change much faster than its culture can respond. When that happens, you can see why the task of radically changing a company's culture is often identified as one of the most difficult challenges faced by corporate leaders.

It is a challenge that is not always successfully navigated. Think of AT&T in its prime. Today, the bluest of the blue chips exists in name only after being acquired by SBC Communications in November 2005. Why did AT&T fall? Because its leaders and employees could not adjust to a world in which long-distance telephone service, the company's cash cow for many decades, was destined to become a low-margin commodity. Other companies have fared better than AT&T, but their culture-changing journeys are never easy. IBM crashed on the reef of its product-based culture and almost sank before Lou Gerstner found a way to reshape it. United Parcel Service, Inc. (UPS) also floundered on its reef of reliable, but nonresponsive service until Oz Nelson reoriented the company's culture.

A major reason why IBM and UPS have so successfully weathered the storms of change and competition is that their leaders wisely enticed them to adopt customer-driven cultures. These cultures are performance-based and primarily focused on the customer's results. They are the same kind of cultures that are overwhelmingly present in the companies and sales forces that business customers identify as world-class sellers and that they support with their buying behaviors.

How can you identify a company whose culture is customer-driven? Certainly, it has to "talk the talk," but many companies that are not particularly customer-driven do that. It must also "walk the walk." Customer-driven companies are always focused outward rather than looking inward at themselves and/or their products and services. They are always thinking in terms of customer needs and desires, and how they might satisfy them. Their primary measures are based on the results they generate for their customers and on long-term customer satisfaction, and they compensate their employees based on those measures.

World-class sellers demonstrate this customer-first orientation in the targets of the improvement initiatives they choose to pursue. Usually, these projects are aimed externally at improving the customer's experience and results rather than at internal operating efficiencies and cost cutting. Consider, for instance, financial services powerhouse JPMorgan Chase & Co., which was an early adopter of on-boarding for customers. It used the technique to bring its new clients up to speed as quickly and efficiently as possible. In the process, the company cut the cycle time required to provide full service to new customers by 80 percent.[94]

Customer-centric companies tend to adopt sales systems that are driven by customer needs. AT&T Middle Market, which boasted an exceptionally successful sales force that was one of company's bright spots, used a "Stewardship Agreement" to help its salespeople define and detail their customers' expectations, needs, and desired level of service. This was a structured mechanism used to "push" the account executive to develop a needs analysis with the customer and "pull" the customer into the process of developing and monitoring the agreement. The agreements explicitly stated how AT&T was going to add value to the customer's business and were used to review products, services, and the added-value benefits delivered. The Middle Market team entered into stewardship agreements with approximately 25 percent of its key customers.

World-class business-to-business sales organizations usually position their salespeople as business consultants rather than product presenters. When we benchmarked the sales force at Boise Cascade Office Products, we found sales representatives flowcharting customer internal processes to identify potential improvements in their purchasing patterns. The sales force was also trained to use a sophisticated activity-based costing system to help customers analyze the exact points in their processes at which their highest costs were incurred.

Customer-driven sellers also utilize service level agreements (SLAs). SLAs use a shared risk / shared savings strategy to create win/win partnerships with customers. They blur the traditional lines between buyers and sellers by setting cost-savings goals that benefit both parties. The customer usually gets a lower initial price, and if the promised goal is reached, the vendor is paid a set fee or a percentage of the customer's savings. Pharmaceutical distributor Allegiance Healthcare, a Chally world-class sales award winner that has since been acquired by another company, used SLAs to underwrite customer projects aimed at reducing inventory and labor costs. When the customer's costs fell below the level preset in the SLA, Allegiance and its customer shared the savings. When costs exceeded their targets, Allegiance shared the added expense.

A final clue to a customer-focused culture is the company's willingness to educate and train the customer's employees in areas that can enable them to improve their company's results. Allegiance Healthcare offered biannual executive leadership symposiums for its key accounts. It also invited its customers' administrative and operating-room personnel to multiday classes to learn about new marketplace trends and new products. General Electric is another standout in this regard. We have already discussed the company's "At the Customer, For the Customer" initiative. It is interesting to note that it was Motorola that first introduced Six Sigma. However, the quality strategy did not spread throughout corporate America until General Electric adopted it and began training its many customers to use it to enhance their own companies.

How Does the Company Segment Its Markets?

I f you explore the histories of major business-to-business sellers, you will see that they were usually founded on the basis of a single product or service aimed at a highly focused group of customers. As these sellers expanded, so did their customer bases. Soon, they found themselves serving such a diverse customer list that they had to organize their customers into addressable groups. They segmented their markets.

Sellers use a variety of segmentation options, including organizing around the customers' industry, size of company, geographical location, technology needs, complexity, regulatory requirements, and the products and/or services typically purchased. The organization of their sales forces is usually derived from and aligned with their segmentation strategy. Both can tell you a lot about the depth of a company's commitment to customer focus as well as its potential for future growth.

The world-class sellers we have benchmarked segment their customers in various ways, but almost all of them share a common objective: they segment in an effort to maximize their ability to provide local service and solutions that best match their customers' needs. For instance, customers with complex global businesses often require levels of expertise and service that can only be achieved through a team-based selling approach. General Electric Industrial Control Systems (GE ICS) established approximately twenty local customer teams to support complex accounts throughout the Americas. Each team, comprising up to seventy members, was run by an advisory board, representing sales, operations, technical functions, a business development leader, and an engineering manager. The advisory board established the team's sales strategies and tactical plans, as well as allocated and positioned its resources to best serve its customers.

Since health care is so highly regulated and the regulations vary so widely, Allegiance Healthcare focused its sales organization on its customers' regulatory environments. For example, when the state of California became a front-runner in the area of managed cost, Allegiance provided health-care systems with alternative purchasing plans designed to reduce and sometimes even eliminate product costs for its customers in that state. It also helped customers respond to California's environmental regulations by reducing product packaging. By redeploying its resources to deal with local needs driven by regulatory laws, Allegiance was able to better understand its customer's problems and provide value-added solutions.

AT&T's Middle Market business unit was established in January 1995 specifically to address a previously unaddressed customer segment: midsized corporate customers spending between $5,000 and $85,000 per month on phone and data services. In addition to creating a dedicated sales force for these customers, Middle Market further segmented them into four geographic regions served by twenty-four sales branches.

The organization of the Middle Market sales force illustrates another commonality in world-class sellers—they are decentralized in order to stay as close to and respond as quickly to the customer as possible. Middle Market pushed authority down the ladder by giving account executives and local managers considerable autonomy in decision-making and pricing. In fact, 90 percent of its pricing decisions were made in the field. Support services, too, were pushed down to the branch level to speed customer response.

Another clue to a company's capabilities is in how well it manages its national accounts. One of the core problems sellers face with national accounts is that they are sold at the corporate level, but serviced at multiple points on a local level. This often results in internal conflicts and service gaps that can hinder the delivery of customer value. The best sellers create mechanisms that enable cooperation across all of the decision points that affect the customer. For instance, Boise Cascade Office Products established an integrated network to sell and service its larger national accounts. One customer contract is negotiated centrally and then, within the network, national account managers work closely with the local field representatives to ensure that service, product, and pricing agreements made with the customer are fulfilled as promised.

Finally, market segmentation involves more than organizing just to sell; it also involves organizing to sell profitably. World-class sellers recognize that successful segmentation requires that they rationalize their marketing and sales expenditures by investing in those segments with the highest growth and return potential and conserving resources in low-potential segments. When we studied IBM, we found that it was employing both face-to-face and telephone sales coverage to optimize its resources. Customers who did not prefer or require face-to-face contact were shifted to an inside team of 600 client and specialist sales representatives who did everything a field rep was capable of handling. The reallocation of customers according to this segmentation significantly increased sales productivity.

How Efficiently Does the Company Adapt to Market Changes?

Change is one of the few constants in business today. The changes inherent in advances in technology, shifting demographics, market consolidation, excess capacity, and global competition all impact business-to-business sellers and their customers.

Those sellers whose ability to change is restricted by bureaucratic structures and sluggish decision-making often see opportunities and sales evaporate almost as rapidly as they appear. Their competitors fill the demand, or new requirements surface and their customer's needs change again before they can react. Conversely, the same conditions can create golden opportunities for those business-to-business sellers who react quickly and capitalize on emerging and rapidly evolving customer needs.

Historically, smaller companies were the most adept at turning on a dime and making quick adjustments and decisions. This flexibility gave them a considerable advantage in the niche marketplaces they served. Today, even the largest sellers are embracing and accepting change as the norm. They are adjusting and responding to market change more quickly than ever. Add it all together and the picture is clear: the ability to continuously improve performance and the flexibility to adapt to protean markets are critical qualities in any company that aspires to become a world-class business-to-business seller.

Companies on the cutting edge of market change are proactive adapters, not reactive responders. Instead of putting out fires for their customers, these sellers are fireproofing their businesses with innovative initiatives. United Parcel Service, Inc. (UPS) has demonstrated this ability repeatedly in the past decade. It was the first shipper to allow its customers to track their shipments—a service that is now commonplace. As supply chains stretched around the world, it created a new, fast-growing service parts logistics business. In 2003, its much-heralded supply chain unit instituted "Flex Global View" that, among other things, sends customers alerts when their shipments are delayed, another first in its industry.

World-class sellers develop "performance" cultures to enhance their ability to adapt and respond. They empower decision-making close to the customer, minimize bureaucratic delays, and reduce cycle time overall. They make a formal commitment to reduce process steps and eliminate unnecessary points of approval to enhance their business process. As we mentioned earlier, Allegiance Healthcare adapted to the fast-changing needs of the health-care industry and the marketplace complexity compounded by various state regulatory requirements by reorganizing to enhance its response, service quality, and speed. AT&T Middle Market, Boise Cascade Office Products, GE ICS, and IBM are all world-class sales award winners that reorganized in order to push decision authority out to customer-facing units.

AT&T Middle Market facilitated decision-making and response by focusing on the more efficient collection and circulation of market data. In a variation on Wal-Mart's weekly market intelligence meetings, Middle Market's branch managers and headquarters personnel participated in biweekly, two-hour telephone conferences designed to share information, solve problems, and recognize and celebrate victories. Since all decision-making functions were represented at the teleconference, many problems were resolved immediately.

Victor Mendes, general manager of sales and distribution at GE ICS, cut through to the frontlines of change by personally calling his salespeople. "I make random calls to our account managers," he explained. "When contact is made, I begin asking questions. 'Where are you? Who did you call on today? How did the call go? Who are you seeing tomorrow? How many new customers are you going to see this week? How many new customers are you going to see next week? What can I do to help? Tell me three things that will make your life easier and enable you to sell more.'" It is a deceptively simple tactic that enhances internal communication and the open exchange of information, and expedites decision-making.

Both business customers and their vendors are recognizing that partnerships are another way to enhance their ability to adapt quickly. Accordingly, buyer-seller partnerships now exist on some level at most companies. Research shows, however, that the majority of these business partnerships fail. The successful ones are those that encompass mutually shared values, vision, business results, and of course, trust and accessibility.

One way that trust is developed is through the open exchange of data. Boise Cascade Office Products provided very detailed account data to its customers relevant to their buying habits and the associated costs. IBM addressed the issue of accessibility by assigning dedicated client representatives to its large-volume partners. In some instances, the client representative was located in the customer's facility, promoting a daily exchange of information, ideas, and solutions. At Allegiance Healthcare, formal quarterly reviews with customers were a standard process, particularly with its partner accounts. During this process, the customer and the Allegiance account management team reviewed the customer's purchasing patterns by product, analyzing the costs with an eye toward continuously adding value.

How Are Customers Served by the Company's IT Initiatives?

In the fast-changing world of information technology, applications change so rapidly that committing them to print tends to be an exercise in obsolescence. Nevertheless, the principle of utilizing IT in the quest to learn more about customers and markets, enhance and empower the sales process, and better serve customers remains perennially relevant. Indeed, over the years that we have been studying world-class sellers, it is becoming an ever-greater priority.

World-class sellers create a competitive advantage through IT by mining and managing customer data. Well aware of the speed of change at the leading edge of IT and the difficulties inherent in capturing the value of IT applications, these sellers tend to be highly skilled in the design, implementation, and management of information systems. Further, their IT systems often become growth engines that drive their results.

Sales leaders hone their customer focus through the collection and dissemination of customer information, product/ service specifications, and purchasing data. At IT's most basic levels, it is facilitating transactions and streamlining administrative duties, and thereby enabling salespeople to spend more face-to-face time with customers. IT also enhances the management of customer relationships and serves as a vehicle for sales training.

We often see world-class sellers using IT to become total solutions providers to customers. The information derived from these applications helps salespeople to define solutions and uncover opportunities for adding value that are not always apparent or easily achieved through the manual review of transactions and questioning customers. For example, GE ICS mined its order database to identify customers in a specific market segment that were still using motors that were more than fifteen years old. The company designed a program to analyze the inefficiencies of those older motors, calculate the associated costs, and compare them to the cost of purchasing new motors. The sales force provided this service to the customers, and earned replacement sales in the process.

Boise Cascade Office Products implemented a variety of IT applications to store, sort, and analyze its customer data. We have already mentioned the activity-based costing software that enabled its salespeople to analyze their customers' processes (directly assigning more than 90 percent of the associated costs, and creating sales opportunities based on hard savings). The company's data warehousing application provided a detailed view of customers' transactions and purchasing patterns and became a cornerstone of the account planning process. Boise Cascade also created a software application named SAVE, which helps customers optimize their office supply usage. It helped the company win the business of a major hospital buying group. Using SAVE, the group was able to compare the costs of the various buying options it planned to offer its client hospitals, which allowed it to conclude that Boise Cascade was the vendor best able to assist in the development and implementation of its purchasing processes.

World-class sellers tend to be enthusiastic adopters of new IT offerings, but they are also fully cognizant of the challenges inherent in successful implementation. We saw this characteristic in action when sales force automation (SFA) first emerged as a highly promising new application. Many sellers rushed into implementations hoping to enhance the productivity of their sales forces. Instead, they often unintentionally automated ineffective processes and alienated their salespeople and customers. Conversely, world-class sellers took a very deliberate approach to SFA. While many sellers were experiencing implementation failures, two-thirds of the best-in-class sellers we studied were devoting additional time to understanding the full ramifications of the technology. They concentrated their efforts on the planning stage of adoption, developing explicit plans that defined their desired end-states, barriers to be removed, process issues to be addressed, and investment criteria.

As always, the world-class sellers oriented their SFA applications toward their customers. For instance, IBM, which created an opportunity management system, applied automation to the process of matching services and solutions to its customers' desired business results. This application automatically specified the resources the sales rep needed in order to successfully sell, implement, and service the best solutions for the prospective customer. It also had the capacity to review the skills, knowledge, industry experience, and proficiencies needed to support the customer, as well as identify a team capable of developing the best solution for the customer.

In addition to orienting IT toward the customer, world-class sellers also devote a good deal of time to the "people" component of IT adoptions. They "sell" their customers and their salespeople on the use of information technology by focusing on its utility and user friendliness, because they understand that the best technology in the world will go unused if it is not easily accessible.

How Evolved Are the Company's Sales, Service, and Technical Support Systems?

T he transformation of salespeople from transaction managers with product-based service and technical support responsibilities into business agents and consultants who are focused on customer results has created a sea change in their day-to-day activities. Further, in order to fulfill customer expectations for personal accountability, advocacy, problem resolution, and the other capabilities that predict world-class sales success, salespeople have less time than ever for transactional and administrative processes.

Of course, this does not mean that these processes can be ignored. Rather, world-class sellers are finding new and creative ways to fill the voids created by the shifting responsibilities of salespeople. Leading sellers are addressing this challenge by building systems into their sales infrastructure that tap into the combined intelligence of the organization instead of depending solely on the talent of the user.

These systems include specialized centers of excellence that bolster the individual salesperson's ability to provide total solutions and manage the results delivery process. For instance,

AT&T Middle Market used data network specialists and a toll-free twenty-four-hour technical support line to support its salespeople. Allegiance Healthcare's range of specialized resources was particularly extensive. Financial analysts monitored regional economies and helped account managers and their customers understand developments that could impact their businesses and purchasing behaviors. Information service specialists provided technical support to the sales force and counseled customers on their IT issues. Marketing liaisons analyzed product data, such as usage trends and pricing options, to ensure that salespeople could offer customers the most attractive solutions. Customer service reps monitored and addressed transactional issues. The resources Allegiance extended to its sales force and customers even included specialized assistance in logistics and the management of receivables and payables.

Successful sellers also intently focus on reducing cycle time throughout the sale. In our studies, we have often found world-class sellers using a TQM-based approach to improving the internal processes associated with sales. GE's much-reported Six Sigma initiative is a notable example. Boise Cascade Office Products employed regional quality managers who were assigned to improve all of its sales-related processes. This focus on process improvement extends into customers' organizations. Allegiance Healthcare created the Procedure Based Delivery System, in which Allegiance's experts studied customers' value chains through to the end users of its products. One aim of these studies was to learn how to prepackage medical supplies in the proper quantities for just-in-time delivery to the point of use.

We have also seen an intense focus on the reduction of the time required to complete routine sales-related transactions. In 2005, carpet manufacturer Beaulieu Group, whose major customers include The Home Depot and Lowe's, equipped its 250-member sales force with order-entry software. Previously, salespeople wrote orders at the customer site and then entered them into the company's system on their return to the office. The orders were then transmitted to clerical staffers who entered them once again into the company's order-processing system. Now salespeople use mobile devices to enter the order directly from the customer site. The change gives salespeople more time to sell, reduces costs, and speeds the delivery of orders to customers.[95]

Finally, we often see world-class sellers developing proprietary infrastructure systems that enable them to apply their core competencies externally. These sellers are encouraging customers to utilize the seller's expertise to improve their business results. Customers of GE ICS, for instance, were offered the Customer Access Node, a technical hotline service that enabled customers to electronically connect their process control systems to a GE-based monitoring center. The monitoring center analyzed and diagnosed the customer's control system remotely.

Allegiance Healthcare turned its core competency in logistics into a proprietary, value-added customer service. The company's logistics team consulted with customers to improve the customers' supply management processes. Sometimes this included taking over the management of customers' storerooms on the customers' premises; sometimes the storerooms were literally relocated to an Allegiance facility. When we studied the company, its western region had more than ninety of these so-called ValueLink contracts in which hospitals' supply rooms were outsourced off-site.

How Does the Company Solicit Customer Feedback and Measure Customer Satisfaction?

The economics of customer retention and the profitability of long-term customer relationships should be obvious by now. We know that the cost of gaining a new customer is exponentially higher than that of expanding business relationships with existing customers. We also know that it is more effective to build market share by putting the customers' needs first than it is to attempt to achieve market dominance through a product-based strategy. These findings support the compelling need for sellers to understand their customers more intimately than ever before.

World-class sellers understand that establishing customers as the primary drivers of strategy and profit requires knowing how their customers' businesses operate, the objectives that are driving their actions, and their unique motivations. These sellers realize that they cannot create solutions that truly provide added value to customers without this knowledge. Accordingly, they create mechanisms that enable and enhance the two-way flow of communication between their customers and themselves.

The best sales organizations generate robust information flows by measuring satisfaction and soliciting feedback at multiple levels within their customers' companies. They are consistently applying and continuously refining their data-gathering processes in order to generate relevant and actionable levels of detail. They also tier the intensity and breadth of their measurement processes according to the importance and value of their customers.

The measurement tools that sellers use range from surveys to complex face-to-face evaluations. Sometimes, we see this feedback process taken to the highest levels of the seller's company, such as when customer advisory boards, patterned after boards of directors, are established and made privy to the seller's business plan and strategies.

When we studied IBM, we found that the company had a dedicated department focused solely on monitoring customer satisfaction. To ensure the integrity of its results, the company went so far as to hire a third party to select the research firms used to gather customer data. At that time, all of IBM's many customers were surveyed annually. The surveys tracked a variety of metrics including overall satisfaction, the rep's knowledge of the customer, the quality of the solution and the sales transaction, the efficiency and quality of the installation process, and the capability and speed of technical support, among others. The resulting findings were benchmarked against IBM's prior performance ratings, as well as the performance ratings of the company's major competitors.

One trend we see among world-class sellers is the extensive effort that they make to involve their customers in the establishment of measurement categories and the review of performance. They know that customer satisfaction is very difficult to measure and that without specific and accurate performance criteria, the feedback process will often provide misleading information. Both Boise Cascade Office Products and AT&T Middle Market directly involved customers in determining the criteria to be used to measure and evaluate their performance. GE ICS informed its drive to be more responsive to customers with a survey program that was designed to identify its customers' priorities. The results of the surveys were used to create a ranked list of Critical to Quality factors that the company then addressed according to their priority.

Of course, information is of little use unless it is communicated and acted upon. The difficulty with most customer feedback programs is that they are typically so lengthy that months will pass before the data is compiled and tabulated and customer concerns are finally surfaced. Nothing is gained by raising an issue and failing to address it promptly. In fact, it can cause irreparable damage when customers believe that their complaints have been heard, yet nothing changes.

GE ICS used Field QMI (quick market intelligence), a market-focused variation on Jack Welch's famous Work-Outs, to enhance its ability to act on customer findings. The company conducted twenty QMI events each year. In each, a wide variety of customer problems were identified and discussed by participants ranging from ICS's CEO to key staff members, regional sales and service managers, and local field team members. The night before a field event, a group of roughly forty people would organize themselves into two- to four-member teams and review the accounts of a preselected set of prospective and existing customers. The following morning, each team reported its key findings and, with the entire group, brainstormed ways to establish or improve the customer relationship. Near the end of the event, a global teleconference, which included up to 200 open lines to relevant field and home-office personnel, added more resources to the mix. Finally, the general sales manager summarized the lessons learned and announced new or revised action plans. Within twenty-four hours, the company's sales teams were hard at work implementing the findings.

How Does the Company Recruit and Select Salespeople?

W e know that there is an ongoing shortage of properly educated sales candidates. We know that customer-centricity has created a shift in which some traditional sales capabilities have been devalued in favor of new, less common skills. In addition, we know that sales positions have almost never been held in particularly high esteem. For all of these reasons, staffing a sales force so that its overall level of competency and commitment to performance is continuously upgraded is a tremendous challenge.

World-class sellers are constantly searching out the highest-quality candidates that they can find. They recognize the sales traits and skills that best match their customers' buying habits. They understand that different customer segments want and require different sales approaches, and they factor these needs into their recruiting and selection processes. Further, they locate hiring authority and accountability where it belongs—with the sales management team.

World-class sellers recognize that salespeople are not interchangeable cogs in a selling machine. There are various sales roles that require distinct (and often noninterchangeable) traits and capabilities, and they tailor their recruitment and selection criteria to those needs. Their sales managers use a selection strategy similar to that of a winning baseball coach. The best coaches first match the skill of the player to the position, and then align the players' combined skills to create a winning team.

IBM recognized the differences between sales jobs in its hiring process for client representatives and sales specialists. The predominant difference between the two positions was the required level of technical capability. Client representatives were responsible throughout the sales process for driving revenue and ensuring customer satisfaction, and so they needed a trait and skill set more aligned with relationship management. Sales specialists, on the other hand, sold "spot" products requiring greater technical and application expertise.

We often find that the recruitment and selection process is migrating from the centralized hiring function closer to the point of customer contact among world-class sellers. This enables selection decisions that are aligned with individual customer needs, as well as the specific regional needs of targeted markets. When a sales position opened at GE ICS, for example, the regional sales manager worked with the region's human resource manager to fill the job. In addition to the standard requirements for an account manager, the pair also identified the critical skills needed for the particular sales territory assignment.

World-class sellers understand that sales managers cannot effectively evaluate and select candidates unless they are properly trained for the task. At Allegiance Healthcare, where both the distributed and the manufactured product sales forces were further segmented by region, regional directors were responsible for the recruitment, hiring, and training of sales personnel. All directors attended a formal training program that prepared them to manage an extensive selection and interview process. Further, each sales candidate was interviewed a minimum of four times by different regional team members.

The selection process tends to be intensive among world-class sellers. At AT&T Middle Market, candidates without sales experience were asked to undergo a four-hour personal assessment conducted by external resources. The assessment focused on resiliency, as well as fact-finding, prioritization, preparation, and presentation skills. Candidates with sales experience participated in a one-hour assessment process, usually conducted by internal personnel. A team-based interview process was favored at AT&T Middle Market. Sales managers were trained in interviewing techniques, and this process was conducted at the individual branches. Interviews were semistructured and example-based, following a competency model that was developed using a focus group of the company's best account executives.

Finally, world-class sellers are increasingly focused on hiring experienced salespeople in order to reduce the ramping time inherent with new recruits in complex sales environments. There was a time when customers were expected to break in new salespeople. They trained them, showed them around, told them what they needed to do. *Not anymore.* Customers no longer have the time, personnel, or motivation to orient new salespeople. If a salesperson is not the knowledgeable resource that the customer expects, that customer will go over the salesperson's head or will turn to a more experienced competitor. The responsiveness that highlights an organization's ability to recognize and adapt to customers' changing needs is significantly enhanced by hiring experienced individuals who are able to hit the ground running.

With a 15 percent to 18 percent turnover rate, Allegiance Healthcare was hiring between fifty and seventy sales representatives each year. Rather than expect inexperienced recruits to quickly master the complexities of its markets and customers, Allegiance shifted its selection process to identify and favor candidates with a demonstrated understanding of the complex sale, the health care industry itself, and specifically, how hospitals and hospital buying groups function.

How Does the Company Train and Develop Its Sales Force?

The fact that business customers identify the effectiveness of salespeople as the most influential factor in their decision to buy makes the importance of this final question for identifying world-class sales organizations exceedingly clear. If individual sales effectiveness is the leading factor in sales success, then sales training and development plays a critical supporting role in that success.

Today, the answer that is not acceptable to the training and development question is "more of the same." Much of the traditional training content—particularly, hard-selling skills that worked for years—are inadequate in today's business-to-business sales environments. Traditional sales-skills training programs and product familiarity seminars will not suffice in the quest for world-class success. Instead, sellers who strive to become world-class must focus on training and development as an ongoing and essential strategic and tactical business process. This process must be one of continuous needs evaluation and re-evaluation designed to identify and close the gaps between the skills and competencies of the sales force and the demands of the marketplace.

As with recruitment and selection, the need to align training to the customer requires that the function be pushed out into the field. When we first started studying world-class sellers, that requirement often meant that sales managers were taking responsibility for skill development through a process of one-on-one coaching. Boise Cascade Office Products, AT&T Middle Market, and GE ICS all actively involved their sales managers in the ongoing education of the sales force. Ian Patrick, Boise Cascade Office Products' sales training and development manager, told us, "BCOP is putting greater emphasis on sales managers having a passion to develop their people." And we found that almost one-third of Boise's seventy district sales managers were running training seminars themselves. The company also added a new management program designed to teach sales managers the basics of coaching. One of its goals was to get managers to approach their work differently, to think more about teaching rather than just directing.

The accelerating trend toward wider spans of control and higher salesperson-to-supervisor ratios is making one-on-one coaching impractical. Nevertheless, sales managers still have an important role to play in defining, selecting, and overseeing training and development activities. That is the only way in which the localized skill gaps that prevent individual salespeople from reaching their highest potential can be identified, measured, and filled.

One aspect of the training and development issue that remains highly stable and relevant is the need for training content that is focused on the customer's business. Business customers continue to look to their vendors for ever-greater levels of technical and applications expertise. This is often a substitute for knowledge that customers previously maintained in-house, or it is a core competency that the customer lacks and is looking to the seller to provide. In any case, it requires more than product knowledge to fill these customer demands. As we have seen, empowered salespeople meet that challenge by understanding their customers' businesses and the markets into which their customers sell.

GE ICS restructured its training program with an eye toward fulfilling this demand. "[T]raining does not stand alone, but fits in with the strategic initiative of the business and management," Jim Panzl, a local customer and team training manager, told us. "We are trying to develop a sales force that is not there just to sell products; they are there to sell productivity to the customer, to improve the customers' revenue stream, or to take the costs out of their customers' businesses. A headliner in training is changing the mindset and developing business expertise and sensitivity. To develop business skills, our account managers need to understand how our business functions and how a customer can impact our business, along with certain financial measurements. We have instituted some simulations in which people can learn and practice these business skills and thereby impact business results within their customers' operations."

At Allegiance Healthcare, the corporate training department offered a broad array of quarterly training to salespeople. This training included topics that were typically delivered to management, such as business processes and programs, financial, P&L, facilities management, conflict resolution, and logistics. The company's regional and branch offices also shared ongoing sales-training responsibilities. New hires spent time in the regional headquarters to understand how the business works, the role that headquarters played, and administrative requirements.

Allegiance's branches provided training programs on issues relevant to the local market, with an in-depth focus on specific products, systems, and services required for customers within that particular territory. "At least once a month, we go into depth on some topic, e.g., cost management," explained regional director Mac Brown. "We try to focus on how the topic impacts the customer and Allegiance by discussing how it drives the economics for each of them. We try to link the impact on the customer and on Allegiance so every time our people make a decision, they consider both sides—the 'win-win' for both organizations."

World-class sellers are increasingly addressing the efficiency, accessibility, and utility of training in an effort to ensure that all salespeople can obtain the educational resources they require to maximize their performance. If training is to be continual—a necessity in the fast-changing business-to-business markets—the traditional method of formal classes alone is too inefficient and time-consuming.

IBM addressed this need with a process designed to manage the ongoing development of its sales forces' skills. When client representatives or sales specialists exhibited a skill deficiency, they were offered a variety of learning activities designed to close the gap. The training was not always mandated per se, but there was an implicit expectation from managers that employees would actively participate in these skill development opportunities. There was also a corresponding expectation that managers would support employees in their pursuit of those activities.

Finally, world-class sellers are just beginning to respond to the necessity of training salespeople to operate as team members and team leaders rather than as independent entrepreneurs. Today's business-to-business sellers are providing system-oriented solutions and custom bundles of products and services designed to address specialized customer needs. Where a customer or market is large enough, team selling is the best way to manage this integration of benefits. In some cases, these customer-driven sales teams are temporary groups created specifically to solve a unique customer problem. In others, as in Procter & Gamble's Wal-Mart team, they are dedicated, independent teams, which permanently manage all aspects of a major customer relationship. In either case, there has been a significant increase in the demand for team selling, even though specific training in the dynamics and day-to-day management of teams continues to lag behind the growth curve.

Epilogue

Sales excellence is a highly ambitious goal, but it is achievable. It requires a salesperson whose personal talents and skills match the selling environment in which he or she works, a solid grounding in traditional and non-traditional sales skills, and, most important in today's highly competitive business-to-business markets, a customer-centric approach.

This last prerequisite of sales excellence has been this book's main theme and the focus of its content. We hope that it has helped you to see your work from your customer's perspective, because that's the perspective that ultimately controls the decision to buy as well as the sales success of you and your company.

Looking back over the seven customer rules and the roles and skills that you must master, it is easy to see that some readers might focus too intently on the challenges of the journey to sales excellence and choose instead to stay on the traditional path to sales success. We hope you won't succumb to that temptation. There is no future in it.

Instead, we urge you to focus on the opportunity to differentiate yourself from your competition and supercharge your results. Remember that salespeople who have mastered all of the skills described in this book are exceedingly rare. So, every step that you take toward fulfilling the customer rules moves you another step ahead the pack and another step closer to world-class status in your customers' eyes.

If you are just beginning your journey to sales excellence, the first three rules will offer the best return on your time and effort:

- *"You must be personally accountable for our desired results."*
- *"You must understand our business."*
- *"You must be on our side."*

These three rules account for a lion's share of the sales success you can earn by selling with the customer's perspective in mind. In assuming the role of the business agent, the CEO, and the advocate and expediter, you establish yourself as one of an elite group of sales leaders.

When you have mastered the first three rules, or if you are already achieving some success selling from the customer's perspective, turn to the last four rules:

- *"You must bring us applications."*
- *"You must be easily accessible."*
- *"You must solve our problems."*
- *"You must be innovative in responding to our needs."*

These are the rules that will refine and extend your skill set in working with customers. Master them and you will lift yourself to a place among the best salespeople in the business-to-business world. In doing so, you will surely guarantee yourself a lifetime of sales success.

As a final thought, we hope that you will always remember that your customers see *you* as the most influential factor in the sale—not the price or the quality and features of the product or any other factor. If you fulfill and exceed your customer's expectations, nothing and no one will be able to undermine your success.

Endnotes

CHAPTER 1

1. Thomas Ginsberg, "Drug Sales Slipping Away," *Philadelphia Inquirer*, December 4, 2005.
2. Christopher Elliot, "Détente in the Hotel Bed Wars," *New York Times*, January 31, 2006.
3. John T. Gourville and Dilip Soman, "Overchoice and Assortment Type: When and Why Variety Backfires," research paper, 2005, 28.
4. Jeff Thull, *Mastering the Complex Sale* (Hoboken, NJ: J. Wiley & Sons, 2003), 189.
5. Holly Dolezalek, "2005 Industry Report," *Training*, December 2005.
6. The effectiveness of this program is demonstrated by the fact that employers, who will otherwise hire only experienced salespeople, hire Ohio University Sales Centre candidates directly upon graduation.
7. Griffe Witte, "Reuters to Move Editorial Jobs from U.S. and Europe to India," *Washington Post*, August 10, 2004, E1.
8. Eric Bellman and Nathan Koppel, "Legal Services Enter Outsourcing Domain," *The Wall Street Journal*, September 28, 2005, B1.

CHAPTER 2

9. Peter F. Drucker, *The Practice of Management* (New York: Perennial, 1986), 37.
10. Benjamin B. Tregoe and John W. Zimmerman, *Top Management Strategy* (New York: Simon & Schuster, 1980).

11. Robert Tillman and Michael Indergaard, *Pump and Dump* (New Brunswick, NJ: Rutgers University Press, 2005), 55.

12. Douglas Brinkley, *Wheels for the World* (New York: Penguin, 2004), 181–182.

13. Clayton Christensen, *The Innovator's Dilemma* (Boston: Harvard Business School Press, 1997), Chapter 9.

14. Fred Reichheld, *The Ultimate Question* (Boston: Harvard Business School Press, 2006), Chapter 5.

15. Strativity Group, Inc., "2005 Customer Experience Management Study," *www.StrativityGroup.com*.

16. Ernst and Young, "Fortune 1000 Buyer Survey" (2002), 3.

17. Mike Judd, "Survey Shows Skepticism on ROI Calculators," *Network World*, March 31, 2003.

18. "Poll Results," *InformationWeek*, November 28, 2005.

19. Deloitte Consulting LLP white paper, "Pursuing Profit," *www.deloitte.com*, 2005.

20 Nike, Inc., "FY 04 Corporate Responsibility Report," 4.

21. Gary Hamel and C. K. Prahalad, *Competing for the Future* (Boston: Harvard Business School Press, 1994), 203–204; and "The Core Competence of the Corporation," *Harvard Business Review*, May–June 1990, 79–91.

22. Richard Freeman, "The Great Doubling," a speech in The W. J. Usery Jr. Lecture Series on the American Workplace, Georgia State University, April 8, 2005.

23. Linda Cohen and Allie Young, *Multisourcing* (Boston: Harvard Business School Press, 2006), 6.

CHAPTER 3

24. Theodore M. Levitt, *The Marketing Imagination* (New York: Free Press, 1986), 128.

25. The processes are described in detail in Neil Rackham, *SPIN Selling* (New York: McGraw-Hill, 1988); Jeff Thull, *Mastering the Complex Sale* (Hoboken, NJ: J. Wiley & Sons, 2003); and Michael T. Bosworth, *Solution Selling* (Burr Ridge, IL: Irwin Professional Pub, 1995).

26. "Best Buy Accelerates Customer Centricity Transformation," corporate press release, May 3, 2004.

27 Don Peppers, "Customer Acquisition Makes a Comeback," *Inside 1to1*, November 14, 2005.

28. Frederick F. Reichheld and W. Earl Sasser, Jr., "Zero Defections," *Harvard Business Review*, September–October 1990, 105.

29. W. Earl Sasser, Jr., and Thomas O. Jones, "Why Satisfied Customers Defect," *Harvard Business Review*, November–December 1995, 88.

30. Joseph Nocera, "Chicken Hawker," *New York Times Magazine*, December 25, 2005, 34.

31. Gartner Symposium's Mastermind Keynote Interview, ITxpo, Orlando, Florida, October 18, 2005.

32. Emmanuel Chéron, et al., "Antecedents, Consequences and Mediating Roles of Trust in Relationships Between Buyers and Suppliers," Sophia University Institute of Comparative Culture Working Paper Series, 2002.

33. Don Peppers and Martha Rogers, *Return on Customer* (New York: Doubleday/Currency, 2005), 53.

34. Anne Mulcahy, World Business Forum, Los Angeles, March 29, 2005.

CHAPTER 4

35. Federal Trade Commission, *Annual Report to Congress for FY 2003 and 2004 Pursuant to the Do Not Call Implementation Act on Implementation of the National Do Not Call Registry*, September 2005.

36. Dana Ray, "Best of the Best," *Selling Power*, January/February 1999.

37. Ellen K. Murphy, "The Presence of Sales Representatives in the OR," *AORN Journal*, April 2001; and Lisa Rapaport, "Pacemaker Sale on eBay Spotlights Dangers," *Sacramento Bee*, March 12, 2005.

38. Theodore Kinni and Al Ries, *Future Focus* (Milford, CT: Capstone, 2000), 198–199.

39. Graham Bannock, et. al., *The New Penguin Dictionary of Business* (London, U.K.: Penguin Books Ltd., 2002), 260–261; and John

P. Kotter and James L. Heskett, *Corporate Culture and Performance* (New York: Free Press, 1992).

40. "Finance for Sales" Web page, *www.intellexis.com/finance_for_sales.htm.*

41. *www.sec.gov/edgar/searchedgar/webusers.htm.*

CHAPTER 5

42. Bill George, *Authentic Leadership* (San Francisco: Jossey-Bass, 2003), 85;and Bill George, "Why It's Hard to Do What's Right," *Fortune*, September 29, 2003.

43. Don Oldenburg, "Demonizing the Customer," *Washington Post*, November 13, 2005, F5.

44. Michael Hammer, *Beyond Reengineering* (New York: Harper-Business, 1996), 4.

45. Glen Urban, *Don't Just Relate—Advocate* (Philadelphia: Wharton School Publishing, 2005), 11.

46. Ibid., 18.

47. Steve Ulfelder, "Do You Really Need a Customer Czar?" *Darwin Magazine*, May 1, 2001.

48. "Faster Food," GE Web site, *www.ge.com/stories/en/20408.html.*

49. Diane Brady, "Will Jeff Immelt's New Push Pay Off for GE?" *BusinessWeek*, October 13, 2003.

50. Stephen Taub, "Bristol's Former CFO Indicted," *CFO.com*, June 17, 2005.

51. From the Henry Fielding translation of Aristophanes' *Plutus* (1742).

52. Dana Ray, "Best of the Best," *Selling Power*, January/February 1999.

53. "Amygdala," *www.wikipedia.com.*

54. Wayne E. Baker, *Achieving Success Through Social Capital* (San Francisco: Jossey-Bass, 2000), 1–2.

55. Allan R. Cohen and David L. Bradford, *Influence Without Authority* (New York: J. Wiley & Sons, 1990), 23–24.

CHAPTER 6

56. James B. Stewart, "The Matchmaker," *The New Yorker*, August 20 & 27, 2001, 78; and Nadine Heintz, "Sales: What Works Now," *Inc.*, June 2004.

57. Mack Hanan, James Cribbin, and Herman Heiser, *Consultative Selling* (New York: American Management Association, 1970), 16–19.

58. Jeff Thull, *Mastering the Complex Sale* (Hoboken, NJ: J. Wiley & Sons, 2003), 135–136; and George W. Dudley with John F. Tanner, Jr., *The Hard Truth about Soft-Selling* (Dallas, TX: Behavioral Sciences Research Press, 2005), 6.

59. Gerhard Gschwandtner, "World-Class Sales," *Selling Power*, January/February 1998.

60. Holly Dolezalek, "2005 Industry Report," *Training*, December 2005, 10.

61. Gerhard Gschwandtner, "World-Class Sales," *Selling Power*, January/February 1998.

CHAPTER 7

62. *www.aa.com/jenkins.*

63. Proudfoot Consulting, "2005 Proudfoot Productivity Report," *www.proudfootconsulting.com/Default.aspx?id=213202*, 25.

64. Dana Ray, "Best of the Best," *Selling Power*, January/February 1999.

65. Kenneth J. Gergen, "Cell Phone Technology and the Challenge of Absent Presence," *www.swarthmore.edu/SocSci/kgergen1/web/page.phtml?id=manu32&st=manuscripts&hf=1.*

66. Steven Levy, "(Some) Attention Must Be Paid," *Newsweek*, March 27, 2006, 16; and Linda Stone, "Your Attention Please" Panel, opening address, SuperNova 2005, San Francisco.

67. Valarie A. Zeithaml, A. Parasuraman, and Leonard L. Berry, *Delivering Quality Service* (New York: Free Press, 1990); Leonard A. Schlesinger and James L. Heskett, "The Service-Driven Service Company," *Harvard Business Review*, September–October 1991, 71.

68. Jay Conrad Levinson, Mark S. A. Smith, and Orvel Ray Wilson, *Guerilla Trade Show Selling* (New York: Wiley, 1997), 238; and Jody Hornor, *Power Marketing Without Money*, Chapter 4, *www.marketingaction.com*.

69. Chris Selland, "Sales Effectiveness: Helping Sales Sell," Aberdeen Group report, June 2004, 1–2.

70. Michelle Bradford, "Vendor Families Propel Region's Shift to Affluence," *Arkansas Democrat-Gazette*, February 5, 2006; and "A Post-Modern Proctoid," *The Economist*, April 12, 2006.

71. "2005 Proudfoot Productivity Report," *www.proudfootconsulting.com/Default.aspx?id=213202, 25*.

72. Dana Ray, "Best of the Best," *Selling Power*, January/February 1999.

73. Rudy Giuliani's address at the World Business Forum, Los Angeles, March 30, 2005.

74. David H. Maister, "The Psychology of Waiting Lines," in John A. Czepiel, Michael R. Solomon, and Carol F. Surprenant, *The Service Encounter* (Lexington, MA: Lexington Books, 1985), 113–123.

CHAPTER 8

75. Mark Thill, "Face-To-Face Still Sells," *Repertoire*, September 2000; and Mark Thill, "Customers Come First for Sales Leaders," *Repertoire*, June 1999.

76. Thill, "Face-to-Face Still Sells."

77. Dorit Wenke and Peter A. Frensch, "Is Success or Failure at Solving Complex Problems Related to Intellectual Ability?" in Janet E. Davidson and Robert J. Sternberg, *The Psychology of Problem Solving* (Cambridge: Cambridge University Press, 2003), 121.

78. Victor Newman, *Problem Solving for Results* (Brookfield, VT: Gower, 1997), 25.

79. William J. McEwen, *Married to the Brand* (New York: Gallup Press, 2005), 82.

80. Anne Mulcahy's address at the World Business Forum, Los Angeles, March 29, 2005.

81. James T. Ziegenfuss, Jr., *Organizational Troubleshooters* (San Francisco: Jossey-Bass, 1988), 26–27.

82. Kevin Reilly, "Auto Manufacturers Can Save Millions by Reducing Defect Detection-to-Correction Time" AMR Research press release, December 5, 2006.

CHAPTER 9

83. Tom Smith, "Software Career Paradox," *InformationWeek.com*, April 13, 2006.

84. Paul McDougal, "Chase Cancels IBM Outsourcing Deal," *InformationWeek*, September 15, 2004; Ed Frauenheim, "Sears Ends $1.6 Billion Deal with Computer Sciences," *CNETNews.com*, May 17, 2005; and Leslie Stroope, "Diebold Cuts Short a Contract with Deloitte Affiliate," *Crain's Cleveland Business*, May 17, 2006.

85. Kenneth M. Landis, et al., *Calling a Change in the Outsourcing Market*, Deloitte Consulting, April 2005, 5, 21.

86. Thomas M. Koulopoulos and Tom Roloff, *Smartsourcing: Driving Innovation and Growth Through Outsourcing* (Avon, MA: Adams Media, 2006), 13.

87. *Expanding the Innovation Horizon: Global CEO Study 2006*, IBM Global Business Services, 2006.

88. Larry Bossidy and Ram Charan, *Confronting Reality* (New York: Crown Business, 2004), 172.

89. J. Nicholas Hoover, "About Face," *InformationWeek*, March 6, 2006, 37–51.

90. Tom Weakland, "2005 Global IT Outsourcing Study," DiamondCluster, 14.

91. Steve Barth, "Knowledge Brainstorming," destinationKM.com, July 6, 2001.

92. Charles Butler, "Dow Corning's Extreme Makeover," *CRM*, June 2004, 30.

PART FOUR: EIGHT QUESTIONS

93. The five award winners were Allegiance Healthcare, AT&T Middle Markets, Boise Cascade Office Products, General Electric Industrial Control Systems, and IBM Corporation.

QUESTION 1

94. Online case study, *www.singularity.co.uk/customers-featured-case-studies-jpmorgan.asp.*

QUESTION 5

95. Elena Malykhina, "Beyond Contact Management," *Information Week*, October 3, 2005.

About The HR Chally Group

For more than a quarter century, organizations around the world have used The HR Chally Group to identify and evaluate the talent needed to differentiate themselves in the marketplace.

HR Chally was founded in 1973 by a grant from the Department of Justice with the goal of creating a *predictive* and non-discriminatory assessment system to prepare for the coming EEOC (Equal Employment Opportunity Commission) legislation.

Through the creation of actuarial databases and statistical algorithms (the technology used by the insurance industry), Chally was able to develop an objective and *predictive* system for identifying effective law enforcement officers. This nondiscriminatory and predictive core assessment set is now backed by more than thirty years of research and a database of more than 300,000 sales, management, and professional employees. To date, Chally has completed more predictive validation studies than all other assessment companies combined. Chally has developed one of the most advanced expert systems built into a sophisticated IT platform and Internet portal. With a single online assessment per candidate or incumbent, Chally collects 866 data points, and can capture an individual's "Work" DNA, to accurately predict competence in 156 distinct work skills and abilities, across more than fifty key business positions.

In an ever-changing business environment, this also requires gathering research from *the customer's point of view.* More than 80,000 in-depth customer interviews form the foundation of Chally's World Class sales force research. Only Chally has remained committed to conducting research on this parallel track—asking customers to objectively "rate" their salesperson on a broad set of competencies, correlating those ratings with their actual buying decisions and statistically identifying the *specific skills* that differentiate top sales performers from weak performers. Chally leads the research in defining the "new sales professional."

Today, more than 2,500 organizations in thirty-five countries and twelve languages have trusted Chally to provide skills assessment and research services in the areas of Talent Management, Leadership Development, and Sales Improvement. Chally clients have experienced *typical* bottom-line improvements including at least 35 percent increased productivity per individual, 85 percent accuracy in identifying "high potentials," and a reduction in turnover of at least 25 percent.

INDEX